LEGENDS OF THE BUFFALO BILLS

Marv Levy, Bruce Smith, Thurman Thomas, and Other Bills Stars

RANDY SCHULTZ

SPORTS
PUBLISHING

Sports Publishing books may be purchased in bulk at special discounts for sales promotion, corporate gifts, fund-raising, or educational purposes. Special editions can also be created to specifications. For details, contact the Special Sales Department, Sports Publishing, 307 West 36th Street, 11th Floor, New York, NY 10018 or sportspubbooks@skyhorsepublishing.com.

Sports Publishing® is a registered trademark of Skyhorse Publishing, Inc.®, a Delaware corporation.

Visit our website at www.sportspubbooks.com.

10 9 8 7 6 5 4 3 2 1

Photos courtesy of the E.H. Butler Library Archives and Special Collections at Buffalo State College with the exception of the following: pages 92, 113, 122, 125, and 127 courtesy of AP/WWP; pages 5, 11, 29, 41, 43, 111, 115, 129, 139, 143, and 144 by Janet Schultz; and pages 59, 61, 63, 65, 71, 99, 101, 103, 105, 107, 115, 131, 132, and 133 by Bill Wippert.

Library of Congress Cataloging-in-Publication Data is available on file.

Cover design by Zach Arlan
Cover photo credit AP Images

ISBN: 978-1-61321-775-7
Ebook ISBN 978-1-61321-789-4

Printed in China

To my family.

Karla, a great daughter, wife, and mother. I'm so proud of you and your accomplishments.

Scott, a wonderful son-in-law. Thanks, too, for your 20-year career in the Army. Thank you for your service to our country.

Damian and Christian, two of the most wonderful grandsons a "papa" could ever ask for.

Finally, my wife Janet. I couldn't ask for a better wife, partner or friend in life. You have always been there for me. I love you.

I love all of you. Thanks for your continued support.

CONTENTS

LEGENDS OF THE BUFFALO BILLS

INTRODUCTION

IT IS HARD to believe that I have been writing about professional football for almost 40 years. I began back in 1976 and didn't realize at the time that nearly four decades later many of those early athletes I interviewed then would be a part of my book today.

As a freelance sportswriter I consider it a privilege and honor to cover the National Football League. For almost four decades I have never taken this privilege for granted.

You have to understand that as a freelancer I am considered like a "hired hand" for each story I'm assigned. I do not work fulltime for any particular media outlet.

So many thanks go to Bills Senior VP of Communications, Scott Berchtold, for honoring my requests over the years for press passes to cover Bills games at Ralph Wilson Stadium, as well as interviews with selected players.

During this time I have interviewed many Bills players as well as people working for the organization. I have considered each one special and enjoyed each story I've been told.

What I did with this book is to try and tell the history of the team with selected players from each Bills era.

I would like to thank a lot of people in helping me make this book possible. First, to *"Shout!" Magazine*, a magazine dedicated to covering the Buffalo Bills. Many thanks to Larry Bump, David M. Jones and Brian Spindler for giving me the opportunity to write a weekly Bills column entitled, "Where Are They Now?"

Second, to the people at Buffalo State College and the E. H. Butler Library Archives and Special Collections for many of the photographs used in this book.

To my wife, Janet, who is always there with encouraging words of support. She also had the privilege of photographing the Bills on the sidelines at the Ralph for 10 seasons.

To editor Julie Ganz at Skyhorse Publishing, many thanks for all your wonderful editing skills. Thanks, too, for making that initial contact with me regarding another book I was involved with. You have been wonderful and very easy to work with.

To Skyhorse Publishing, many thanks for allowing a guy from Wilson, New York, to do a rewrite on a Bills book that had been originally published 12 years ago.

Finally, to those of you reading this book. I found out a dozen years ago just how powerful a book on the Bills can be with their fans. At the book signings I attended, I appreciated each and every one of you who bought the book.

I also enjoyed the conversations I had with each of you, no matter how short or long each one may have been.

I have found out through my travels across this great country of ours that there are many great sports cities. But I don't think there is one quite like Buffalo, with the love affair their fans have with their Bills.

Football is truly a way of life for Bills fans, no matter how passionate or casual a fan they may be of the team. It is something that can be felt 12 months a year, 365 days a year, 24/7. That excitement is once again building with new owners, Terry and Kim Pegula (see the final chapter in this book).

They are not only improving the Bills on the field but building the enthusiasm level up for the city of Buffalo as well as Western New York area, something that has not been seen in these areas in years.

It is truly an exciting time to be a Bills fan as well as a Western New Yorker.

To all of you, thank you and enjoy.

1960
BUFFALO BILLS

WITH EVERY ORGANIZATION, you need a solid foundation. The foundation for the Buffalo Bills came in 1960 when that first team took the field. Although they may not have had a great first season, they became the base from which a great organization evolved.

That is how retired Bills athletic trainer Ed Abramoski remembered that first Bills team, which began play in 1960.

It began as a dream. Nineteen sixty marked the beginning of a new decade. It was a year that saw U.S. pilot Francis Gary Powers shot down while flying over the Soviet Union in his U-2 plane. Adolf Eichmann, the infamous Nazi war criminal, was captured in Argentina, and John F. Kennedy would edge out Richard Nixon for the American presidency.

But on July 30, 1960, a crowd of 16,474 at Buffalo's War Memorial Stadium watched the Boston Patriots defeat the Buffalo Bills, 28-7 in a preseason opener that served as the first game in American Football League history.

Since that night, 43 years have passed, and during that time the Bills have evolved into one of pro football's most successful franchises.

"I remember the first day we arrived for our first training camp in East Aurora," said Abramoski. "The football helmets didn't come in until six o'clock the night before we were to begin practice. The equipment man and I stayed up all night putting the facemasks on and getting those helmets ready."

The late Dick Gallagher was the general manager of the Bills. He hired Garrard "Buster" Ramsey as the team's first head coach. Ramsey assembled a staff of assistant coaches that included Harvey Johnson and Floyd "Breezy" Reed.

OPPOSITE:
Ed Abramoski

BUFFALO BILLS

Ramsey, who coached the Bills in their first two seasons in the AFL, recalled those first years in the fledgling league.

"It was really difficult, a tough deal, starting up a new team in a new league," stated Ramsey. "Besides coaching, I did a little bit of everything. I helped order and select our uniforms and other equipment we used. And I really didn't know anything at all about Buffalo. I had come from Detroit. But I soon found out just how good a football town Buffalo was. The fans were tremendous, especially in that first year I was there."

Ramsey had one other memory from his Buffalo days.

"That training site we used in that first year out in East Aurora, where they had the polo fields on the Knox estate, was awful," remarked the former Bills head coach. "It was like practicing on concrete. The surface was that hard."

Then there was the team itself. Four individuals tried their hands at quarterback that first year, including John Green, Tommy O'Connell, Rich Lucas, and the late Bob Brodhead. Lucas was the Bills' first draft pick ever. He became part of pro football trivia.

"I was a pretty good defensive halfback," said Lucas, who played his college football at Penn State. "But I just wanted the chance to quarterback a team. I had more of an opportunity to do that in Buffalo. So I signed with the Bills and never regretted it."

Lucas remembered that first training camp held at East Aurora. "Buster Ramsey and his coaching staff were really working very hard, but they didn't have the best conditions to work in," said Lucas. "There were so many people trying out that it was almost impossible to figure out who was coming and who was going in that first camp."

But Lucas appreciated the fact that Ramsey gave him a chance at quarterback.

"Tommy O'Connell and John Green were the main quarterbacks that year for the Bills," recalled Lucas. "And they got sacked a lot that first season. The offensive line that was playing in front of them was weak.

"But Buster gave me my chance to show what I could do. But it wasn't easy. I had trouble learning the cadence or calls that a quarterback had to do. And I know that Buster was really frustrated with me because of that."

Green remembered that first year.

"It was a wide-open league," stated Green. "The league was made up of either rookies or veterans. There didn't seem to be too much in between."

Green made history on October 23 when he led the Bills to their first regular-season home win ever, 38-9, over the Oakland Raiders. Green threw for 243 yards and four touchdowns and ran for another.

"Running back Wray Carlton is the guy who made me look good that day," remembered Green. "He scored three touchdown passes from me on a day that was very rainy and muddy. And on most of my passes to him, Wray was the secondary target. He would just catch the ball and run with it after he caught it. Wray did most of the work."

Green had the Bills' first 300-yard passing performance the following week when Buffalo beat the Houston Oilers, 25-24. It also marked Buffalo's first two-game winning streak.

Green would end up that initial season leading the Bills in touchdown passes (10), yards passing (1,267), passes attempted (228) and completed passes (89).

Besides Carlton in the backfield, other Bills running backs included Fred Ford, Wollmer Fowler, Darrell Harper, Joe Kulbacki, Harold Lewis and Carl Smith. The offensive line consisted of offensive tackles Tony Discenzo, Ed Meyer, Harold Olson and Bob Sedlock. Offensive guards were Phil Blazer, Don Chelf and Ed Muelhaupt. Dan McGrew was the center.

The wide receivers included Bob Barrett, Dick Brubaker, Dan Chamberlain, Monte Crockett, Al Hoisington, and Tom Rychlec.

The defensive front line included Leroy Moore, Charlie Rutkowski, Lavern Torczon, Mack Yoho, Gene Grabosky, Chuck McMurtry, John Scott and Jim Sorey. The linebackers had Bernie Buzynski, Joe Hergert, Jack Laraway, Archie Matsos, Sam Palumbo, Dennis Remmert and Joe Schaffer. The defensive backs included Jack Johnson, Billy Kinard, Rchie McCabe, Jim Wagstaff and Billy Atkins.

During many of the Bills' home games that initial year, you could hear fans yell, "Yooooo Ho," each time the home team kicked off. The cheer was for Yoho, who, besides being a defensive lineman, handled many of the Bills' kicking duties, including kickoffs, extra points and field goals.

"I think I got the job through process of elimination," said a modest Yoho, although it may have been true, because he was one of five players to attempt a field goal in 1960.

While Buffalo's offense may have struggled that first year (ranked eighth in the eight-team AFL), the defense shined. Leading the way on defense was Matsos. In that first season, the former Michigan State star had eight interceptions for the Bills.

"That was a strange first year," recalled Matsos. "The Bills had the best defense in the AFL. But they also had the worst offense. I guess the defense that year set the tone for future Bills teams."

The Bills finished their first season with a 5-8-1 record, good enough for a third-place finish in the AFL's Eastern Divison.

But it was just the start for the Bills. Van Miller, who has been the radio voice of the team for 33 of its 40 seasons, summed up that first year.

"We were part of something new and exciting," commented Miller. "We struggled and the team lost money. But it was the start of a love affair between a team and Western New York. It may not have been pretty at times, but it sure was a lot of fun."

And it was just the beginning of an organization that would produce many legendary players over the next 43 years.

RALPH WILSON

"IF IT WASN'T FOR RALPH WIL-son, there wouldn't be a Buffalo Bills team today. He was the guy who brought the team to Buffalo with the old American Football League. He was the guy who stuck it out through those years in the AFL when money was a big factor.

He stuck it out through the years of playing in old War Memorial Stadium, a stadium that had character but was outdated by the time the Bills began playing in it in 1960. He helped get a new stadium built in 1973.

He stuck it out through the good and bad years of the franchise. He never gave up. And today, he's one of the most respected owners in the NFL. He is respected in Western New York and Southern Ontario for keeping the NFL in Buffalo when others would have been happy to see the Bills move elsewhere.

"Ralph Wilson is a giant in the sport."

That is how former Bills athletic trainer Ed Abramoski described Bills owner Ralph C. Wilson Jr., the only owner the Bills had ever had.

Buffalo history in professional football is legendary. A charter member of the National Football League in 1920, Buffalo's stay was shortlived. They would later appear as members of the old American Football League and the All-American Football Conference.

Their stay in the AAFC was for only four seasons before the league dissolved. Three teams from the AAFC were absorbed into the NFL in 1950, including the Cleveland Browns, San Francisco 49ers and Baltimore Colts. Buffalo had been shut out again until Wilson came along in 1959.

OPPOSITE:
Ralph Wilson (left) and Chuck Knox (right).

By the following year, Wilson had reintroduced professional football to Western New York with the formation of the Bills with the American Football League.

Wilson joined Lamar Hunt, along with six other owners, to form the AFL. "The Original Eight" or "The Foolish Club," as they were better known as at the time, included the Bills, Dallas Texans, Boston Patriots, New York Titans, Oakland Raiders, Los Angeles Chargers, Houston Oilers and Denver Broncos.

"A lot of people, including the NFL, really didn't give us much of a chance to survive at the time," recalled Wilson.

But survive they did. Interestingly enough, it was following initial talks between Wilson and Carroll Rosenbloom, then owner of the Baltimore Colts, that a merger with the rival NFL was initiated.

As president of the AFL in 1965, Wilson served on the expansion committee and the AFL-NFL negotiations committee. Over his 44 seasons as owner of the Bills, he has served as chairman of the NFL pension committee and was a member of the labor committee.

He also served on the board of NFL Charities, the Super Bowl policy committee, realignment working group and is actively working on league governance issues.

"There is no doubt in my mind that Ralph Wilson has been a driving force, both in the AFL and in the NFL," recalled a former Bills defensive lineman, the late Tom Day. "If it weren't for Ralph Wilson there wouldn't be a Buffalo Bills franchise."

And like any good owner, Wilson always wanted a winner in Buffalo and did everything in his power to provide the fans with one.

"I don't think a lot of people realize how much money Mr. Wilson pumped into the Bills in those early years in the AFL," said Day. When other teams were losing money, the Bills were one of the few that were making money.

"And when the Bills needed a new stadium, I don't think Mr. Wilson ever intended to move the Bills to any place other than Buffalo. And believe me, if there was anyone who deserved a new stadium it was the Bills."

Another former Bills player from the 1960s, Wray Carlton, agrees.

"War Memorial Stadium served its purpose," said Carlton. "But it was a unique, old stadium. You were very close to the fans when you came on the field. If they liked you, they cheered you. If they didn't, they had ways of letting you know that as well."

But thanks to the efforts of Wilson, the fans of Buffalo have one of the best state-of-the-art football stadiums in the NFL today.

"And I guess you could say that he deserves to have his name on the stadium. He has done a lot to make the Bills one of the premier football franchises. He certainly deserves a lot of the credit for going out and getting the right people to run the organization," Carlton said.

"But even more importantly, he has given so much back to Buffalo and the Western New York community. The hundreds of thousands of dollars he has given to charities in and around Western New York is just one example."

And in many cases, he has done it without a lot of fanfare. Also, he has done a lot for former Bills players who may have been down on their luck a little or had some misfortune hit them.

Wilson was finally recognized for all his efforts on and off the field when he was elected to the Pro Football Hall of Fame on January 31, 2009. He was officially inducted on August 8, with his presenter being ESPN's Chris Berman.

Ironically the next day the annual Hall of Fame Game was played between the Bills and Tennessee Titans (originally the Houston Oilers, an original AFL team). That date would have marked the 50th anniversary of the AFL had the merger between them and the NFL had not taken place.

Sadly, Wilson died less than five years following his induction into the Hall at the age of 95.

Former Bills head coach Marv Levy speaks very highly of the team owner.

"Mr. Wilson is a real friend to not only myself, but to many players, people connected with the NFL, as well as people from

Ralph Wilson

around Western New York," remarked Levy. "Not only did he care about the football team, but the Buffalo area as well.

"There is no question either that he would have loved to have seen the Bills win a Super Bowl. The players wanted to win one for him as well."

STEW BARBER

During his nine-season career with the Buffalo Bills, former offensive tackler Stew Barber started 112 consecutive games. But that's not to say that he necessarily finished them, thanks, in part, to a former defensive end named Larry Eisenhauer.

Barber and Eisenhauer, who played for the Boston Patriots, had some legendary battles against each other over the years in the area known by many offensive and defensive linemen as "the trenches." A few times the battles resulted in less playing time for the duo.

"I remember one game, I can't exactly recall what year it was, my wife had arrived at the game," recalled Barber, who played for the Bills from 1961-69.

"She didn't take her seat right away, and the game was already under way by the time she did. But what had happened in those few minutes was that Larry and I had gotten into a fight in the opening minutes of the game. We were both tossed out. By the time my wife arrived, I was already back in the locker room. She wondered what had happened to me when the offense came back on the field and I wasn't in the lineup."

Barber remembered that the battles he had with Eisenhauer were for real.

"Today, I have a lot of respect for Larry," said Barber. "But back then it was all-out war. It was really physical. We would really go after each other during games. He was the toughest player I ever faced. He was a relentless, tough player.

"We even got into fights in the AFL All-Star Game during practices against each other. And we were on the same team at the time."

Barber was also quick to point out that the Patriots were the toughest team he had to face during his American Football League career. "They had a lot of tough, physical players on their team," commented Barber. "The Kansas City Chiefs may have had bigger players, but they weren't as physical on the inner line. Boston certainly was."

The former offensive tackle addressed the issue of 112 consecutive games and what that signified.

"You have to remember that at that time we only had 33 to 35 players on the roster," stated Barber. "You were expected to play as often as possible. You were simply expected to play, injuries or no injuries.

"And I believe that those that played with injuries had their careers shortened. And many of those players are still paying physically for it today. I really believe that total knee replacements were common for players who played in the era from 1950 to 1970.

"It was after that that money came into the picture and teams took a little more interest in how they treated their players."

Following a distinguished undergraduate career at Penn State, Barber was drafted in the fourth round of the 1961 AFL selection meeting by the Bills. At the same time, the former offensive lineman was selected in the third round of the National Football League Draft by the Dallas Cowboys.

He turned down an offer to play for the Cowboys and came to Buffalo to play for the Bills instead.

"My decision to play for the Bills was based pretty much on geography," stated Barber, who was a five-time All-AFL choice and appeared in five league All-Star Games.

"I was from the East and I liked that area of the country. To me, Buffalo was a bit like home."

Barber has many memories of his playing days with the Bills. He remembers the championship teams of 1964 and 1965.

"It was the defense that made us rise to the top," said Barber. "We had a defense that created chances for the offense. And we had a very strong running game, where we could grind out yardage and eat up the clock."

Barber retired following the 1969 campaign. He stayed in football, first as an assistant coach in the old World Football League with the New York Stars and Chicago Wind. Then he returned to the Bills in 1975 as a scout. He later was an assistant general manager and general manager (1979-82) for the club.

Although he is no longer involved with football, Barber still follows the game.

"It's a different game today," said Barber. "Volumes of money are available. It is more of a business than during my playing time. And when you have that much money, problems may occur. History has shown that you will have disagreements, no matter what business you're in. Football is no different. But it will survive."

BUTCH BYRD

FORMER BILLS DEFENSIVE BACK Butch Byrd will tell you that he was five years old before he realized that his first name was really George.

"My godfather began calling me 'butcher' when he got home from the war," recalled Byrd. "Pretty soon it was simply 'Butch.' That's what everybody called me after that. Until I ran into my kindergarten teacher, who asked me what my name was.

"I told her it was Butch. She said no, it was George. I was so surprised that I had another first name that I ran crying all the way home. But I've been Butch ever since."

Byrd played in the American and National Football Leagues for eight seasons, seven with the Bills (1964-70). Over three decades have elapsed since Byrd last wore a Bills uniform. Yet today he is still the team's all-time leading pass interceptor with 40.

"I think that record really speaks well of itself," said Byrd. "I've never been one to look at records or brag much. But that is a mark that I am very proud of holding. And to think that it has stood on its own for over 30 years is really amazing, considering how records are changing constantly in different sports, including football."

Byrd was drafted in the fourth round of the 1964 AFL draft by the Bills. The NFL Dallas Cowboys selected the Boston University graduate in the seventh round of their draft. It didn't take long for Byrd to figure out who he would sign with.

OPPOSITE:
Butch Byrd (42).

"That was the same year that the Cowboys drafted another cornerback by the name of Mel Renfro in their first round," recalled Byrd. "It didn't take too much to figure out that he would be starting and that I would be just lucky to make their team. So I signed with the Bills."

Byrd found Buffalo to be a city that he really liked.

"My family and I were always treated very well there," commented Byrd. "But that's the way the people there treated their football players. Football is very special in Buffalo. It is important to their culture."

A culture that, in the mid-1960s was undergoing a great deal of change nationally. Racial movements were ongoing in many parts of the country, including Buffalo. In fact, Byrd and teammate Mike Stratton became part of a revolutionary movement in professional football.

"We were some of the first black and white players to ever room together on the road," stated Byrd. "Probably the most famous duo to ever do that of the time was Gale Sayers and Brian Piccolo of the Chicago Bears.

"It was really nothing special to Mike or myself, although we realized what was happening. We accepted it, although there were several members of the Bills team, both black and white, at the time that didn't. But we still roomed together despite any objections."

Byrd and Stratton were part of a powerful Buffalo defense that many football historians feel carried the Bills to their two AFL championships in 1964 and 1965.

"The defense was just outstanding," said Byrd. "Just look at the players. Although none of us were really outstanding athletes, we really worked well together and shut teams down," Byrd said.

"I think the two best examples of just how good our defense really was were the two championship games we played against the San Diego Chargers. The Chargers' offense was as good as anybody's at that time, including the top teams in the rival NFL. But we ended up totally shutting them down. They scored only one touchdown against us in two games. And we shut them out in the '65 championship game."

But Byrd will be the first to admit that he was only as good as the defense in front of him.

"The key to any successful pass defense is the defensive line. And we had one of the best in pro football."

Byrd was also quick to point out that his relationships with his teammates were, and still are, important to him.

"I still consider Jack [Kemp] a good, close friend of mine," remarked Byrd. "Mike [Stratton] and I were the closest of friends. He was probably the closest friend I had on the team. But probably the heart and soul of those Bills teams of 1963 and 1964 was Cookie Gilchrist. When he was traded to Denver [1965] his loss was felt both on and off the field. Especially in the locker room.

"He would challenge people in the locker room to do better. He could really get you worked up. That meant a lot to our guys at that time."

Byrd faced some still competition on offense. Two of the better receivers he had to defend against were Paul Warfield and George Sauer.

"I played against Paul when he was with the [Miami] Dolphins," said Byrd. "He was the best I ever faced, period. He was just a great athlete. He could catch footballs that I sometimes thought were uncatchable. And he did it with such grace and style. There is good reason for him to be in the Football Hall of Fame.

"George, on the other hand, was a guy I had to concentrate on all the time. You just never knew when Joe [Namath, New York Jets quarterback at the time] would throw to him.

"George was very deceptive. He would try and lull you into a safe sense. But he could come up with the big catch when it was needed."

The two things Byrd especially remembers of his days in Buffalo were the fans and War Memorial Stadium.

"There was just a special relationship between the fans and the players," concluded Byrd. "They were very passionate about their team. They cared about the players, especially if they knew that you were trying your best. But they could really give it to you if you didn't. You could hear it from them when you were on the sidelines or coming up the tunnel from the locker rooms. When you came up that tunnel and into the open, you could almost touch the fans, that's how close they were to you.

"But then again, that's how the stadium was designed. I couldn't believe it when I first saw it. It always seemed to be old-looking. But it had character, just like the fans it held."

ELBERT DUBENION

IF SOMEONE HAD ASKED Elbert Dubenion after his first Buffalo Bills game over 45 years ago if he thought he would ever see his name inscribed on the team's Wall of Fame, he would have simply said no.

But as Dubenion and others found out, one game does not make a career. The talented wide receiver played with Buffalo for nine seasons (1960-68). His accomplishments were so great that the Bills honored Dubenion by placing his name on the Wall of Fame at Ralph Wilson Stadium. He was the fifth player at the time so honored.

"Having my name on the Wall has been a long time in coming," said Dubenion. "I really appreciate the honor. I've wondered for a long time if my name would ever be placed up there. This is the greatest honor that I've ever experienced in my football career."

Dubenion's professional football career didn't actually begin until 1960, when he was 27 years old. "Golden Wheels," as he would become known to Bills fans, was signed by Buffalo as a free agent by Bills general manager Dick Gallagher.

Dubenion had played college football at Bluffton College in Ohio. Following that he served a stint in the United States Army and worked for an iron company. Not exactly what you would call Wall of Fame credentials.

While Dubenion may have had the speed of a wide receiver (9.6 in the 100-yard dash), he didn't have the experience.

"I had been a running back," stated Dubenion. "But because I was so fast, Buster Ramsey [the Bills' first head coach] decided to make a receiver out of me. And I think that after the first game he played me as a wide receiver, Buster may have had some second thoughts.

"The one play I remember is a reverse that quarterback Tommy O'Connell ran for us.

Somehow I got caught in the crossover. Two players ran into each other and got hurt. I messed up and thought I was gone. Buster Ramsey really chewed me out for that.

"But I managed to come back and score a couple of touchdowns, which made Buster happy."

Golden Wheels admitted that outside of having his name placed on the Bills' Wall of Fame, his greatest moment as an active player came the first week of September 1960.

"Making the final 33 after the Bills' final roster cut was the greatest moment for me," stated Dubenion. "That was really tough, especially after messing up in that first game. But it was the greatest feeling I ever had in football to know that I was a member of a professional team. I'm glad it turned out to be the Bills."

At one time Dubenion held almost every Bills receiving record. Then came Andre Reed of the Bills of the 1990s, who has virtually put his name on almost every one of those records.

"That Andre Reed is one of the greatest receivers I've ever seen," said Dubenion. "He really did a great job for the Bills and was one of the main reasons the team went to the Super Bowl four straight times in the early 1990s."

Dubenion is also the first to give credit to where credit is due when it comes to the success he experienced with the Bills.

"I didn't do it all myself," recalled Dubenion, who wore number 44 during his playing days with the Bills. "There were times when I first began playing for the Bills that I really didn't want to get hit coming over the middle, especially if I wasn't catching the ball.

"But I soon found out that an opposing player would still take a good shot at you, even if you were going after the ball. That's when I decided to try and catch the ball a little better. And the guy who helped me do that was an assistant coach by the name of Johnny Mazur [a receivers coach with the Bills]. He was the guy who really worked with me and helped me develop good catching techniques."

Duby considers the best season he ever had to be 1964, when he caught 42 passes for 1139 yards, a 27.1 average, and 10 touchdowns.

"That was a great football team we had that year," remembered Dubenion. "We had Jack Kemp and Daryle Lamonica at quarterback. Daryle was polite and would ask me what I wanted as far as a pass went. Jack would just call the plays and you got what he dished up.

"The team itself was a great one. Maybe one of the greatest ever. I guess they just don't get enough recognition."

Dubenion has received the recognition.

"I'm just glad to have survived that final cut," concluded Dubenion. "At the age I was at, I just wanted to take it one year at a time. I'm just glad to have stayed on a long as I did. I enjoyed every minute of it."

COOKIE GILCHRIST

WHEN IT COMES TO DESCRIBING Cookie Gilchrist, you could sum it up in one word: unique.

That is how the late Tom Day once described former Buffalo Bills running back, Carlton Chester "Cookie" Gilchrist. Day, a defensive lineman who played with Gilchrist when the two were together with the Bills, remembered Gilchrist, the person and player.

"There was never any doubt that Cookie walked to the beat of his own drum, so to speak," said Day. "He was his own man.

"He gave the Bills a powerful running attack during the three seasons [1962-64] he played in Buffalo. There weren't too many guys who could stop Cookie once he got up a full head of steam running.

"I saw the great Jim Brown play for the Browns and I saw Cookie. To me, they were equal. I think there were some who would say that Cookie might have been a little better.

"If it hadn't been for his character, which was a bit controversial at times, and the fact that he played part of his career in the Canadian Football League and the rest in the American Football League, I think people would have looked a bit differently at him. All I know is that he was one powerful running back, and I'm glad I didn't have to face him that much during my career."

Another Bills teammate at the time who knew Gilchrist pretty well was fellow running back Wray Carlton.

"There is no doubt that Cookie was one of the leaders on our team during that era," recalled Carlton. "He was one of those punishing running backs.

"I can remember watching him play against some of the biggest defensive linemen in the AFL at the time and watch them bounce off of Cookie as they tried to tackle him. It was just unbelievable."

Gilchrist stood 6'2" and weighed 243 pounds during his playing days. He joined the Bills for the 1962 season. He had just finished playing his third season in the CFL. He had been banished from the league for disciplinary problems.

Buffalo head coach Lou Saban looked past those problems and took on Gilchrist. One of the more memorable contests Gilchrist played in occurred on December 8, 1963.

On that day the Bills crushed the New York Jets, 45-14, at War Memorial Stadium. But the big news of the game came from the fact that Gilchrist had rushed for 243 yards on 36 carries, setting a new all-time pro football record. On top of that he scored five touchdowns to set an AFL and Bills team record.

"There was no stopping Cookie in that game," said former Bills backup quarterback Daryle Lamonica. "He was just on a roll. It was an important game for us as well because we were in a battle for the AFL's Eastern Division crown with the Boston Patriots," Lamonica said.

"We just kept wondering how much he could take. I think he proved how much punishment he could take, as well as dish out, in that game. He was a one-man wrecking crew."

Offensive tackle Stew Barber remembered Gilchrist. "Cookie was very special in his own right," stated Barber. "He was a very big, physical player. To me, Cookie was 15 years ahead of his time as a player. I think he could have fit into playing football in the 1980s and 1990s.

"Cookie was so good, he could have been a linebacker and a fullback and would have been an All-Star at both positions. And I think he could have played both positions, if given the chance to be the iron man. Cookie was a tremendous blocker. He could take a defensive end and throw them aside with no trouble at all. He was very strong."

But the following season, coaches, players and fans got to see what Gilchrist could be like if he didn't get his own way.

In one particular game in 1964, November 15 against the Boston Patriots, Gilchrist became upset at the Bills' play calling during the game. So in the middle of the action, the star running back stalked off the field, called in his own substitution, and headed for the dressing room.

An outraged Saban cut Gilchrist two days later and put him on waivers. But cooler heads prevailed. Quarterback Jack Kemp, sensing that the Bills were very close to winning the AFL title, talked Saban into taking Gilchrist back. But that came only after Gilchrist apologized to Saban and the rest of his teammates.

"It was a very critical point in our season," said Lamonica. "We knew that we needed Cookie and a solid running game in order to take the AFL title."

"Cookie actually played a pretty complete game that day," recalled Kemp. "He did a little bit of everything that helped our attack out. We ran on the ground, threw through the air and cut off the Chargers' offensive attack with our defense. It was a convincing victory."

"Cookie was so good, he could have been a linebacker and a fullback and would have been an All-Star at both positions. And I think he could have played both positions, if given the chance to be the iron man. Cookie was a tremendous blocker. He could take a defensive end and throw them aside with no trouble at all. He was very strong."

—BILLS OFFENSIVE TACKLE STEW BARBER

Things were tense for a few days, but Kemp worked things out between Cookie and Lou. And it was a somewhat humble Cookie who addressed his teammates a few days later. The apology was accepted.

The Bills finished the '64 campaign with a 12-2 record. The only team that stood between them and the AFL title was the San Diego Chargers.

Before a packed house at War Memorial Stadium, the Bills crushed the Chargers, 20-7. The game is best remembered for the hit on Chargers running back Keith Lincoln by Bills linebacker Mike Stratton.

But the fact can't be overlooked that Gilchrist ran for 122 yards on the ground that day and combined with Carlton to rush for over 200 yards between them. And when he wasn't running the ball, he was throwing some devastating blocks to protect Kemp.

Unfortunately for Gilchrist it was his last hurrah in a Buffalo uniform. Before the 1965 season began, Saban had traded Gilchrist to the Denver Broncos.

"It came as quite a shock when we traded him," said Lamonica. "But it was pretty much felt by management that no player was bigger than the team. And while we managed to win another AFL title and two more Eastern Division titles, our running game was never the same."

There was nobody quite like Cookie when it came to dynamic running.

Gilchrist was finally recognized for his outstanding football career in the latter years of his life. He was inducted into the Greater Buffalo Sports Hall of Fame in 2011 following his death.

Gilchrist died of cancer in early 2011 while living in an assisted living facility in Philadelphia, Pennsylvania.

PETE GOGOLAK

WHEN YOU LOOK AT PLACE KICK-ers in the NFL these days, you notice most are soccer-style kickers. There are very few kickers in pro or college football today who kick straight on.

It wasn't always that way. Back in 1963 there were no pro sidewinders. But the following year a young man name Pete Gogolak introduced soccer-style kicking to the world of pro football as a member of the Buffalo Bills.

"Everybody was skeptical about soccer-style kickers in those days because there weren't that many," remembered Gogolak. "I went to Cornell University and played football with their team. And naturally I kicked soccer style.

"I remember when Bills scout Harvey Johnson came to see me. I don't think he had much faith in my style of kicking either.

But he came by after one of our practices. He told me to get a bag of footballs and kick them. I did and I guess I proved my point because the Bills drafted me 13th in their draft. I was very happy to be getting the chance to play pro football.

"The NFL didn't even draft me. I was totally ignored by them."

But that changed two years later when Gogolak became a pioneer again. He was the first player to ever jump from the AFL to the NFL when he joined the New York Giants in 1966.

Despite spending most of his pro football career with the Giants, Gogolak has many fond memories of Buffalo and the Bills.

"I really loved Buffalo, both the city and the team," remarked the Hungarian native. "The best teams I ever played for were the Bills in 1964 and 1965. Those teams were better than any I ever played on with the Giants.

"We really had some good players, like Cookie Gilchrist, Jack Kemp, Elbert Dubenion and Mike Stratton. I was really happy in Buffalo. We were the toast of the town. I remember even having to shovel snow to help clear the field one year," Gogolak said.

"That would not be something you would see today. But that's how things were back then. We all pitched in together to take care of things for the game. I must admit that I even enjoyed that. But I made up my mind to leave because I couldn't come to terms with [Bills owner] Ralph Wilson. I played out my option. I didn't sign a contract my second season, took a ten percent pay cut, and played for $9,900 that year.

"About a month before my contract ran out, the Bills tried to sign me. But by that time it was too late. I had already made my decision. The Giants' offer tripled what I made with the Bills. So I took the chance and I jumped leagues. I guess that caused quite a furor in the AFL. But there were no hard feelings. The city was good to me, and I'll always appreciate that."

Gogolak admits that he would have remained a Bills player had an earlier offer come in.

"I signed with the Giants for $30,000," remarked Gogolak. "I really didn't want to leave Buffalo. Mr. Wilson could have had me for $20,000."

Several years ago, Gogolak talked about his feelings about free agency coming into the

NFL. While he may have had some concerns, he felt that it was something that could work.

"I grew up in a socialistic system," recalled Gogolak, who fled with his family from Hungary to the United States in 1956. "But I prefer the system here in the U.S. You are free to go where you want. It goes according to supply and demand. In business, it's good to go where you want to go. So I think it should be the same for pro football. I think it should be a free market with players being able to go where they want. And I think you will find the theory of 'the rich get richer' won't really be true. I really believe that kind of system in pro football will work."

Lou Saban (left) and Pete Gogolak

JACK KEMP

JACK KEMP RECALLED THE 1963 Eastern Division playoff game between the Buffalo Bills and Boston Patriots as though it was yesterday.

The Bills lost at home, 26-8, to the Pats, who would go on to play for the American Football League title.

"I remember telling coach Lou Saban as we walked off the field at War Memorial Stadium that those fans who were booing us then would be cheering us next year. I really felt that we had the makings of a championship club and we were just a year away from winning it all."

Little did Kemp realize what a prophet he was, because, as he said, the following year the Bills did walk off the same field as AFL champions. Kemp quarterbacked the Bills for eight seasons (1962-69), as well as a total of 10 seasons in the AFL (1960-69). He was originally drafted by the Detroit Lions in

the 17th round of the 1957 NFL draft. Cut before the start of that season, Kemp would bounce around for three seasons with the Pittsburgh Steelers and New York Giants of the NFL and Calgary of the Canadian Football League before signing with the Los Angeles Chargers of the newly formed AFL in 1960.

Kemp was with the Chargers until midway through the 1962 campaign when he was put on waivers while on the injured reserve list. Because of the foul-up in paperwork by the Chargers, the Bills claimed Kemp for the waiver fee of $100.

"It was the best $100 we ever spent," head coach Lou Saban would say later.

"It also solved our quarterback problems at the time," stated Hall of Fame guard Billy Shaw, a teammate of Kemp with the Bills. "It is the key position of your team and we were struggling trying to find a starter.

"Call it fate, or whatever you want, but when the Chargers messed up their paperwork on Jack, the Bills jumped right on it and signed him. He was the leader we were looking for on offense."

Ironically, by 1963 Kemp found himself in a battle for the starting quarterback position with a rookie by the name of Daryle Lamonica. Lamonica remembers those days with Kemp. He recalled the four seasons he spent backing up Kemp, but coming in several times to relieve the veteran QB and pull a game or two out of the fire for victories.

Many felt there was a feud between the two. But Lamonica said feelings were actually to the contrary.

"I had then, and I still do now, a great deal of respect for Jack Kemp," said Lamonica. "I learned a lot from Jack about quarterbacking. And I truly believe that we were a great one-two punch at the position for the Bills."

While the Bills may have won their first AFL title in 1964, it was their 1965 season that brought out the best in Kemp.

"We really changed our offensive game that year," remembered Lamonica. "In '64 we had depended a lot on Cookie Gilchrist and our running attack to carry us. That was our bread and butter that year. But that all changed in '65. The Bills had traded Gilchrist in the off season to the Denver Broncos. So we went to a pass-oriented game more that season than we ever had before. We not only went to our receivers, but we threw a lot to our running backs. And I really think it brought out the best in Jack that year. Jack was a great quarterback and leader. But I truly believe that he had the best season of his career in 1965. He was one of those players who made a difference for us that year."

Kemp also made a difference for the Bills in other ways as well. In his own way he was becoming a clubhouse lawyer and trying to keep peace on a team that for a couple of campaigns (1963-64) had some troubling times, especially with one running back by the name of Gilchrist.

"Cookie had a mind of his own at times," recalled Lamonica. "Late in the '64 season Cookie didn't like the way plays were being called, especially when it didn't involve him, and in one game decided to quit. So he walked off the field, called in his own replacement, and said he had had enough.

"Actually the guy who had enough was Lou Saban. By the following Tuesday, Lou was ready to cut Cookie. That was, until Jack stepped in. Jack talked to Cookie and asked him if he would apologize to the rest of the team for his actions.

"Then Jack went to Lou to see if he would accept the apology. Everything was worked out, Cookie was back on the team, and they went on to win their first AFL title.

"There was no doubt in my mind that Jack was a good politician."

It was a sign of things to come. By the end of the 1969 season, Kemp had been approached by the Republican Party in Erie

Jack Kemp (center).

County to run for Congress. Following the conclusion of the '69 AFL season, Kemp retired and ran for Congress.

"I had a four-year, no-cut contract with the Bills at the time," said Kemp. "I figured that if I lost I could always come back and play. But the fans had their say and I was elected to Congress."

Kemp became a representative of New York's 31st congressional district. He would spend nine terms in the house. He ran for president, losing out on the nomination, and later became a vice-presidential candidate, losing again.

For nearly four decades Kemp was in the public eye as a public servant. He did so until his death from cancer in 2009.

Despite all of his political endeavors, Kemp still recalled those AFL years very fondly.

"That was a great brand of football," said Kemp. "It was wide open. The fans really enjoyed it and it really opened up the game.

"The AFL was innovative. It was fun to watch and fun to play."

PAUL MAGUIRE

LIKE MANY PEOPLE, Paul Maguire owns several wristwatches. There is one in particular that he wears that can set his mind instantly back to the 1960s, when Maguire played in the old American Football League.

"This watch means a lot to me," said Maguire. "Of the hundreds of players that played during the 10-year existence of the AFL, only 11 of us played the whole 10 seasons. I was one of them. In honor of this achievement, the AFL presented all of us with watches. It is something I will always cherish."

Maguire, who played one season in the NFL's American Football Conference after his years in the AFL, played for the Los Angeles/San Diego Chargers from 1960-63 and the Bills from 1964-70.

Following a brilliant collegiate career at The Citadel that included being chosen an Associated Press All-American, Maguire was drafted by the NFL's Washington Redskins in the 17th round of the 1959 NFL Draft.

"The funny thing was, Washington never contacted me after picking me," recalled Maguire, a linebacker and punter during his playing days. "But Frank Leahy, general manager of the Los Angeles Chargers, did. He called first and then followed up with a couple of other calls. Then he came to see me. After hearing nothing from the Redskins, I signed with the Chargers on Christmas Day [1959] for $9,000, plus a $2,000 bonus. That was big money in those days. It was a lot for me," Maguire said.

Maguire remembered many of his early days with the Chargers and the AFL.

"One of the frustrating things back in the early days was the fact that you could only carry 33

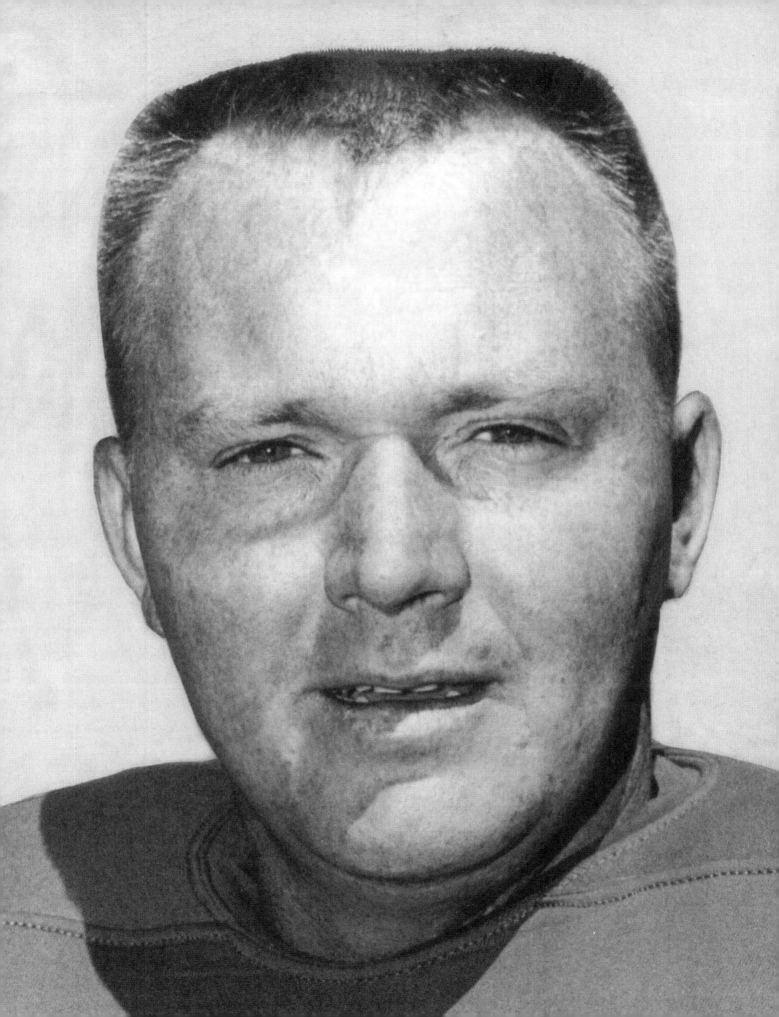

guys on the team," said Maguire, a native of Youngstown, Ohio. "But we had six of the best coaches ever to walk on a football field coaching us that first year and all of whom went on to football success at one time or another."

There were head coach Sid Gillman and assistant coaches Jack Faulkner, Al Davis, Don Klosterman, Joe Madro and Chuck Noll.

"Of course one of the things I won't ever forget were the 18-day Eastern road trips the Chargers took almost every year when we would play Buffalo, New York and Boston.

"But it was fun. We weren't playing for money because no one really made that much. We really became close on the road and did a lot of things together. And we did a little drinking as well."

Following the 1963 season Maguire was cut by the Chargers and picked up by the Bills.

"I didn't appreciate the fact that San Diego had cut me," commented Maguire. "It happened on the last day of training camp, just prior to the beginning of the 1964 season. It really hurt. But I was glad that Lou Saban gave me another chance with the Bills. Of course I got my revenge when the Bills beat the Chargers in 1964 and 1965 for the AFL championship. And we did it so convincingly both times.

"But I'll always remember 1965 the most because we beat the Chargers on their home field for the title and shut them out in the process, 23-0. The other interesting fact about that game was that my wife and Jack Kemp's wife were the only two players' wives in attendance

from Buffalo for that game. This was before all the wives were allowed to travel at the team's expense to a championship game."

Maguire admits that Saban was one of his favorite coaches he ever played for.

"Lou treated you like a man," said Maguire. "He would let you do your own thing. Lou was very easygoing. Everybody respected Lou and liked him a great deal. I don't think I've ever come in contact with anyone who didn't like Lou."

During the course of his career in Buffalo, Maguire saw the AFL grow in respectability.

"The NFL-AFL rivalries were very intense during the mid- and late sixties," remembered Maguire. "Buffalo's Cookie Gilchrist was the best fullback the AFL ever saw and probably the best ever at that position, with the exception of Jimmy Brown. Cookie ran with power and authority. He could really grind it out for you.

"Of course I think anybody will tell you that Joe Namath of the Jets did more for the AFL than anybody. He was a showman, a talker, but most importantly, he produced. And he proved that by leading the Jets past the Baltimore Colts in Super Bowl III."

On the lighter side, Maguire tells of how he used to take issues into his own hands with the Bills.

"One of the biggest complaints I used to have with the Bills was that they used to give me lousy footballs to practice with," says Maguire, now a commentator for ESPN broadcasts of the NFL. "I would get all the

used game balls that weren't good any more. To me it was like practicing with basketballs, because that's how out of shape they were. But nobody ever listened to me. So finally one day I let in a bunch of local kids to our practice with specific instructions and rules to follow. I proceeded to then take all those old footballs and punt them into the waiting arms of those kids who were sitting in the stands. As soon as they caught them, they were off and running out of the stadium.

"After that, I got new footballs to practice with and I never had any more problems."

But problems of a different nature did arise for Maguire and the Bills. Following a dismal 1-12-1 record in 1968, Buffalo hired John Rauch, who had guided the Oakland Raiders to an AFL championship only two years before.

Rauch lasted only two seasons with the Bills, but they were two of the worst ever experienced by Maguire.

"To me, John Rauch was an absolute idiot," quipped the outspoken former punter. "He was on a big ego trip. He wanted to prove that Al Davis [the Raiders' managing general partner] had not really run the team, but that he had. He never proved it with the Bills. He only proved to be a loser. I couldn't believe the way he ran practices either, especially with me. I was alone most of the time. I would practice by myself and then go home.

"The only time I was with the team was on game day or when we traveled. It was strange. Following the 1970 season, I was so fed up with Rauch and discouraged with football in general that I retired. I was 32 when I quit."

GEORGE SAIMES

GEORGE SAIMES WAS NAMED TO the Buffalo Bills All-Time Team during the club's 25th anniversary season in 1984. Back in 1969, Saimes was also named to the American Football League's All-Time Team.

Pro Football Hall of Fame coach Weeb Ewbank then asked the question as to why Saimes wasn't enshrined in the Hall of Fame in Canton, Ohio. If a distinguished coach like Ewbank questions it, why haven't others? Saimes stayed low-key about the situation.

"I've never really questioned it," commented Saimes, who played in the NFL and AFL for 10 seasons (1963-72) with the Bills and Denver Broncos. "It was a great honor to be named to the AFL's All-Time Team. There are a lot of great players on that team. You have to remember that there were a lot of outstanding players that played in the AFL during their 10 seasons of existence.

And it was nice to be named to the Bills All-Time Team.

"I never gave the Hall much thought until I heard about Weeb's comments. Coming from him, it is quite an honor," Saimes said.

The former safety played seven seasons in Buffalo (1963-69) before finishing his career in the Mile High City. Like many Bills fans, his fondest memories were of the Bills' championship seasons of 1964 and 1965.

"Playing on those two championship teams were the highlights of my career," commented the Michigan State graduate. "It would have been nice to play on a third in '66. Actually, we snuck into the playoffs in '66. We just couldn't beat Kansas City in the championship game. It would have been great to go to that first Super Bowl against the Packers. I think we would have matched up better against them than the Chiefs did. But that's history."

Had it not been for a trade when Saimes was drafted, the former defensive back might have been playing for those same Chiefs against the Packers in the initial Super Bowl.

"I had been drafted by the [Los Angeles] Rams of the NFL and the Chiefs of the AFL," recalled Saimes. "K.C. wanted to know that if a deal could be worked out with another team would I sign with the AFL. I really didn't follow the NFL at that time. So they traded me to Buffalo and I became a Bill."

Saimes became part of a defensive unit that, at the time, was considered one of the best in not just the AFL, but in all of pro football. Saimes's mentor was former Bills defensive coach and head coach Joe Collier.

"I was very close to Joe," stated Saimes. "He was great. Joe was one of the finest defensive coaches in the game. He taught me the football that I learned in the pros."

Saimes continued, talking about his days in the AFL.

"Being a safety, I really didn't have that much of a problem," said Saimes. "The AFL game was a wide-open affair. Sid Gillman [coach of the San Diego Chargers at the time] was a man ahead of his time. He created some great offensive schemes, which the rest of the AFL picked up on. The AFL had explosive offenses.

"There were a lot of great receivers like Lance Alworth and Don Maynard. But the guys I had to deal with the most were the running backs coming out of the backfield as receivers. Jim Nance [of the Boston Patriots] was the toughest and strongest receiving back I had to take on. He was extremely powerful. He was a big, thick back. Thank God I only had to face Cookie Gilchrist [former Bills running back] once. When we were teammates I had seen what he had done to other guys on defense. He could destroy you. I only had to tackle him once, and he was already falling when I hit him. But that was enough for me."

The former safety, who had 22 interceptions during his pro career, gave his views of the modern-day pro game.

"I think pro football today is a more wide-open game, even more than during my playing days in the AFL," stated Saimes. "You can have up to four wide receivers moving at one time. And teams are constantly shuffling players in and out of the lineup."

Saimes kept his eye on the Bills.

"They are a team in transition right now," said Saimes. "But what they accomplished over the past decade is amazing. I hope that history will show that they were one of the greatest teams of all time. Winning four straight conference titles is hard to do. People don't realize how hard that was to do."

Just like people don't realize what a great safety Saimes was. Perhaps that history will someday change.

Ironically, Saimes was born and raised in Canton, Ohio, home of the Pro Football Hall of Fame. He made it his home for his entire life.

Known as a battler his whole life, Saimes spent the final years of his life battling leukemia. In one of the few battles he lost, Saimes died of the disease in March of 2013.

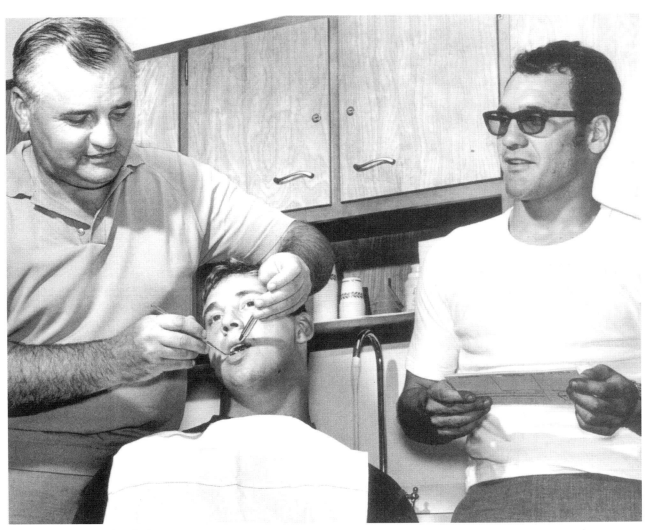

George Saimes (right).

BILLY SHAW

IF THERE WAS A MOMENT that defined Billy Shaw's Hall of Fame career, there are many who will say it came during the week of October 1, 1967.

Shaw, an All-Pro guard and offensive team captain for the American Football League's Buffalo Bills, had torn a knee ligament and underwent surgery back in late July. Less than three months later, following weeks of rehabilitation, Shaw was ready to test the knee.

"I remember it well," recalled teammate Paul Maguire, now a football commentator for ESPN telecasts. "It was a cold and rainy day in October. We all knew that Billy was trying to come back from his knee injury. While most of us could have gone inside after practice, everyone stayed outside in the cold and rain and watched Billy practice. Everyone stayed there to support him, to show him that we cared. That's what kind of

impact Billy had on us as a person and team leader."

Shaw, who played nine seasons with the Bills (1961-69), was elected to the Pro Football Hall of Fame in January 1999 as the lone senior candidate. The former guard was selected with Lawrence Taylor, Eric Dickerson, Tom Mack and Ozzie Newsome. He was only the second member of the Bills to be elected to the Hall. The first was O. J. Simpson, who was selected in 1985.

Although it took him 25 years to be selected, Shaw is glad to be enshrined in Canton, Ohio, at the Hall of Fame.

"I knew already back in August that I would be the lone seniors candidate going to the selection committee," remembered Shaw, who played his college football at Georgia Tech where he was an All-America tackle.

"I knew that I would go to the final seven, and on the day that the announcement was made, it was horrendous. I didn't hear my name at first. It was the last one announced. But what a feeling it was when I finally heard it.

"I cried. I think everyone who was with me that day did, too. This means a lot to me. It's the greatest honor ever given to me. I began playing football when I was in the fourth grade. Now I've achieved everything I've ever gone after. What's really nice is the fact that I'm the first member to enter the Hall who played his entire career with the American Football League. I retired before the team and league were merged with the National Football League," Shaw said.

seven of his nine seasons on the team, he was captain of the offensive unit. It was a job that he was honored to hold.

"It was a position voted on by the team, so that made it even nicer to have," commented Shaw. "And I was captain during an interesting changing period of time in our country's history, especially with the Civil Rights movement.

"You see, being from the Deep South as I was and being raised in Mississippi, I had never played with a black player until I got to Buffalo. That was a whole new experience for me. But I think I handled it well, and I believe that I had the support of the black players as one of the captains of the team."

"Off the field, Billy was one of the most genuine people you would ever want to meet. He got along with everyone. It set the example for the rest of the team. It didn't matter if you were black or white. We all got along. The Bills of that era were a very close-knit team."

—TEAMMATE ERNIE WARLICK

Shaw came to the Bills as a second-round AFL draft pick. He had also been drafted by the Dallas Cowboys of the rival NFL. Shaw elected to play for the Bills and was a first-team AFL selection from 1962-66 and a second-teamer in 1968 and 1969. He was also named to pro football's All-Decade team of the 1960s, as well as to the all-time AFL team.

Shaw was one of the most dominating players to ever wear a Bills uniform. During

As one of the duties as captain of the Bills, it was Shaw's responsibility to bridge any gaps there may have been between players and the coaching staff. One player on the Buffalo squad whom he remembers the most with this situation was the great running back, Cookie Gilchrist.

"Any time you had Cookie on a team, there were bridges to gap," said Shaw jokingly with a laugh. Shaw continued, recalling Gilchrist the player and the person.

"Cookie was one of the best players, not just runner, I ever played with or saw," said Shaw. "He was a smart football player. I can remember the first football preseason game he ever played for us in 1963. He ran the ball, caught the ball, even tried to throw the ball. He wanted to return punts and kickoffs. He was willing to even play some defense and kick the ball if needed."

"He just loved the game so much that he was willing to do anything to help the team. But running is what he did best. And boy, could he run. If you blocked well for Cookie, he could really bust through those holes you made for him. But if you got in his way when he was coming through the line, he would occasionally hit you square in the back coming through. That gave you the incentive next time to block and get out of Cookie's way."

Another teammate who recalled Shaw as a player and person was tight end Ernie Warlick.

"He was one of the best blockers I ever saw," stated Warlick, who played four seasons with Buffalo (1962-65). "If you had those third-and-one situations and the quarterback would ask in the huddle who could move somebody on the defensive line to get us that yard, Billy would almost always pipe up and say he'd do it. And he did.

"Off the field, Billy was one of the most genuine people you would ever want to meet. He got along with everyone. It set the example for the rest of the team. It didn't matter if you were black or white. We all got along. The Bills of that era were a very close-knit team," Warlick said.

Another player for whom Shaw blocked was running back Wray Carlton. "Billy was the hard-nosed competitor who didn't like to get beat," remembered Carlton, who played for the Bills for eight seasons (1960-67). "To me he was a fullback playing guard. I think the greatest moment I'll always remember about Billy was the hole he blew open for me in a 1965 game against the Houston Oilers. I ran through it for 80 yards and a touchdown. And Billy was leading the way for me all the way. I was even having a problem keeping up with him the final ten yards or so. That's how good of an athlete Billy was."

Outside of his election to the Pro Football Hall of Fame, Shaw's greatest moment came in 1964 when the Bills won the AFL championship.

"The guys on the team were young at the time and just beginning to reach their potential," remembered Shaw. "I think Cookie had his best year ever as a running back. Jack Kemp and Daryle Lamonica also had good years. Maybe not their best, as far as individuals go. But the competition that was going on between them for the starting quarterback spot was healthy for the rest of the team. And, yes, I'm one of those people who believe that had we had the chance to play the Baltimore Colts or Cleveland Browns [the runner-up and the champion, respectively, in the NFL], I think we could have given them a good game."

Shaw talked at length about that offensive line that he played on.

"We had a great offensive line that was very close," said Shaw. "There was Joe O'Donnell [guard], Dick Hudson [tackle], Al Bemiller [center], Stew Barber [tackle], Ernie

Warlick [tight end] and myself. We were a very close group. We all played hurt at one time or another and knew it. When one was down, the others would try and help lift their spirits. We tried to lift each other up. You never ended up feeling sorry for yourself in that group. I still admire those people today, especially for the sacrifices they made. Ironically, we all came in at about the same time and all left at about the same time. It was a special time in our lives."

When Shaw as inducted into the Hall, Bills head trainer Eddie Abramoski was charged with introducing him.

"Eddie was there in Buffalo with me the whole time I was there," explained Shaw. "I've also believed that trainers have never gotten the credit that they so richly deserve. Eddie kept me healthy during my career. I have a lot of respect for Abe. He is a close friend."

Maybe Maguire expressed best how he and the rest of his teammates from that era of pro football feel about Shaw going into the Hall of Fame.

"It's like all of us who played in the AFL are going in with Billy," said Maguire. "He was a great leader on and off the field. Everyone had respect for Billy. It was long overdue for Billy. But we're all glad he's in the Hall."

RON McDOLE

MILLIONS OF VIEWERS WATCHED Super Bowl XXVI in January 1992 when the Buffalo Bills played the Washington Redskins. No one had more mixed feelings that day about both teams than Ron McDole.

For 18 seasons (1961-1978) McDole played the defensive line for the American and National Football Leagues, including stints with the St. Louis Cardinals, Houston Oilers, the Redskins, and the Bills. Eight campaigns were spent in Western New York with the Bills. McDole's final eight were with the Redskins.

But McDole handled the situation very diplomatically at the Super Bowl party he attended.

"We took both jerseys with us to the party," stated McDole. "I wore the Redskins' and my wife wore Buffalo's. I also purchased team hats for both teams and sewed them

together. I just kept turning it around and around on my head as the game went along. But I have to admit that deep down I was really pulling for Buffalo because they had never won a Super Bowl. To me, the Bills are still of the old AFL. I really miss the AFL-NFL rivalry. It's not the same today with the AFC-NFC.

"I was sorry to see them [the Bills] lose it again. That's never a good feeling when you lose in a game like this. I know what it's like because I was on the losing side with the Redskins back in 1972 against the Miami Dolphins. It's just one of those situations where you don't get that many shots at a Super Bowl. But when you do, you try to make the most of it," he added.

Which is something McDole did during his 18 seasons of play. What Bills fans remember most about McDole is that he combined his

talents with that of Tom Day, Tom Sestak and Jim Dunaway to form one of the best defensive lines in the history of the Buffalo franchise.

And McDole has even stronger feelings than that about the entire team that he played for.

"We [the Bills] won three straight Eastern Division titles in the old American Football League from 1964 to 1966," remembered the University of Nebraska graduate. "We just missed out on the title in 1963, losing to the [Boston] Patriots. And to top all of that we won the AFL championship back to back in '64 and '65. We had a very strong and dominating team during that time span. The disappointing thing about all of this is that only one player from that era is in the Hall of Fame. Billy Shaw. And there are some other pretty good candidates like Cookie Gilchrist, Tom Sestak, John Tracy, and Mike Stratton, among others.

explain what made those Bills teams so outstanding during those years in the 1960s.

"We were just a very well-balanced team," stated McDole. "We had great players both offensively, defensively and on special teams. And we all worked for one common goal: winning."

The former defensive end explained what made the Bills' defense so good.

"We had confidence in our abilities," said McDole. "If the offense turned the ball over, we knew that we would get it back to them again very quickly."

McDole was also very quick to give a great deal of credit to former Bills coach Lou Saban for saving his professional football career.

"I used to have what was called migraine seizure," commented McDole. "It was the closest thing you could ever get to an epileptic attack. I had started getting these when I

> "We had **confidence in our abilities.** If the offense turned the ball over, we knew that we would get it back to them again very quickly."
>
> —RON McDOLE

"It just bothers me that guys who played for the Houston Oilers and San Diego Chargers, two of the other dominating teams of those early AFL years, are in the Hall and only one Bill is. I just don't understand it," lamented McDole. McDole went on to

was with the Oilers. I would get really bad headaches. And I would react strangely to them. But Saban and the Bills were willing to take a chance on me when other teams wouldn't. I'll always be grateful to Lou for giving me that chance."

The former Bills No. 72 admits that he never expected to have his playing career go on as long as it did after he was traded to the Redskins in 1971.

"Things were changing in Buffalo and it was time for me to get out," recalled McDole. "It was sad to leave Buffalo, but I never thought I would go on to play eight more years. But George [Allen, the Redskins' coach at the time] wanted older players like me. I always loved going after players on the field. And

George was the type of coach who would work the team's defense around our abilities and let us be ourselves."

Although he played until he was 40, McDole still feels that he never really retired from the game.

"I always enjoyed playing the game of football," said McDole. "I was fortunate in that I never got hurt. But maybe a former teammate of mine on the Redskins, Pat Fischer, said it best when he said, 'I didn't quit. They just took the uniform away from me.'

"That's all they did to me to get me to stop playing. Who knows how long I would have gone on if they hadn't taken away my uniform?"

MIKE STRATTON

"MIKE IS LIKE A GUIDED MISSILE.
Once he sets his sights on a ball carrier, he rarely, if ever, misses him. Mike is one of the hardest-hitting players and is regarded as the best pass rusher in the American Football League."

That is how Bills linebacker Mike Stratton is described on the back of his 1966 Topps football card. And no truer words have ever been written.

Stratton played 11 seasons (1962-72) with the Bills and a final campaign with the San Diego Chargers (1973). During his time spent in the American and National Football Leagues, he earned All-Pro honors for six consecutive years.

But what Buffalo fans will always remember about Stratton is what has become known around Western New York as simply "the hit."

It occurred during the 1964 AFL championship game between the Bills and Chargers. San Diego opened the scoring on their first possession.

But the second time the Chargers got the ball, Stratton slammed into San Diego running back Keith Lincoln, putting Lincoln out of the game and sending what the Bills' media guide described as a "ripple" of excitement through the Buffalo stands.

That play changed the momentum of the game toward the Bills, and they eventually went on to defeat the Chargers for their first AFL championship.

That "ripple" has managed to survive the years for Bills fans of that era, and the Lincoln hit has become legendary.

"That play apparently played a significant part of the game," said Stratton, a native of

Tellico Plains, TN. "What was on my mind at the time the play occurred was to find some way to make sure that I was on the field. Unfortunately it had happened once already in that game.

"San Diego had a very explosive offense. On certain plays they would put a back out behind the defense, towards the sideline. They would also move a receiver out the same way, but towards the hash marks. All you would hope to do on defense was to get to the back before the ball did. That's what we were doing on the particular play where I hit Lincoln.

"Thanks to a high throw it worked for me. But it didn't work so well for Lincoln. I gave him a pretty good lick," Stratton said.

Stratton went on to remember those Bills teams of the 1960s, especially the championship years of 1964-66. He recalled the important role the defense played on those teams.

"Throughout football history, every team has had a strong part to it," stated the University of Tennessee graduate. "For the Oakland Raiders and San Diego Chargers it was offense. But for the Bills over those championship years, it was defense. But we have to remember that we could not have won anything without exceptional contributions from the offense. The defense gave the offense what it needed to be successful. And that defense was like a body. Each player had a significant role to play. One was like the heart, another like a leg, a lung, etc. When it worked together, there was no

defense that was better. But when it broke down it could become pretty ugly."

Stratton was the second player the Bills chose in the 13th round of the 1962 AFL draft. Surprisingly, the Bills had selected 12 other players before Stratton, none of whom ever went on to play a major role in the Bills' eventual successes of the 1960s.

Interestingly, the only other player chosen by Buffalo that year who became a star on the Bills of that era was Tom Sestak, picked in the 17th round.

Stratton and Sestak would become the cornerstones of a powerful Bills defense.

"Those were great years during the 1960s," said Stratton. "The championship years of the '60s were the foundation and the establishment of Buffalo as a major football city in North America. I still have a lot of fondness for those times. The joy of playing with the team in the '60s and playing in Buffalo are the two things I remember most."

Although he doesn't follow football as much as he used to, Stratton still appreciates being remembered.

"I'm just grateful to be remembered at all," jokes Stratton. "I have always said that I would like to be remembered as a durable ballplayer who did not make a great number of mistakes and had the ability to come up with a few big plays."

Stratton managed to do that with "the hit."

OPPOSITE:
Mike Stratton goes for the tackle.

TOM SESTAK

IF TOM SESTAK HAD PLAYED in a different era of pro football, he would be in the Hall of Fame today. In fact, if the AFL-NFL merger had come sooner, and a few more people would have seen Tom play, there is no doubt he would have been in the Hall of Fame. Tom was just that good.

Those comments, or ones similar to them, have been made by many of Sestak's former teammates with the Buffalo Bills during their glory years of the mid-1960s, when the team won back-to-back American Football League titles in 1964 and 1965 and three consecutive AFL Eastern Division titles from 1964 to 1966.

Unfortunately the former Buffalo Bills defensive tackle passed away in March of 1986 after suffering a heart attack. It came as a blow and a wake-up call to many of his former teammates. "He passed away long before he should have," remembered former teammate and business partner Paul Maguire. "When Tom passed away many of us gathered to remember him and the fact that we ourselves are mortal. But this shouldn't have happened so soon, not for a guy like Tom, who enjoyed life."

A year after Sestak passed away, the Bills honored the former defensive tackle by placing his name on their Wall of Fame at Rich Stadium.

But who was Sestak? There are many Bills fans who have heard of him, but a generation or two have grown up never seeing this defensive lineman ever play a down.

Sestak came to the Bills as their 17th-round pick in the AFL draft out of McNeese State in 1962. He was quoted as saying at the time,

"My advisors consider the Bills one of the outstanding organizations in pro football, and I feel I will have a good future with the Bills and in the AFL."

And it didn't take long for Sestak to catch the eye of many Bills observers, including their head coach at the time, Lou Saban.

"I like his speed and the way he moves," said a very impressed Saban at the time. "You never know he's out there. He knows his job and he just keeps working."

Sestak was just another piece of the puzzle Saban was assembling that would lead to the beginning of back-to-back AFL titles two years later. Sestak would be joined on the defensive front line by the likes of Jim Dunaway, Ron McDole and Tom Day.

By the 1964 campaign Sestak would become the anchor to a Bills defensive unit that dominated the AFL.

"Sestak was *the* guy on that defense," commented former teammate and now coach of the San Diego Chargers Marty Schottenheimer. "Tom was very strong, very physical and a very, very intense player. He was the big guy on the defense. Unfortunately, it was bad knees that brought his career to an abrupt end."

Which was very true. Sestak played on some very painful knees during his career. But it wasn't enough to stop him from going after quarterbacks and sacking them or blocking field goals or extra point kicks, or even shutting down a team's running attack. And if you got hit by Sestak, he left his imprint on you.

"When Sestak hit you, you knew it," commented former Bills and Oakland Raiders quarterback Daryle Lamonica. "Fortunately, I played most of my career on the same team. But for a couple of years after I went to Oakland I remember having to face Sestak and the rest of my ex-teammates.

"And despite his bad knees, he got to me a couple of times and I knew it. But it was amazing watching him play from the sidelines during his great days with the Bills. I winced every time he got to an opposing quarterback and hit him. He could blitz with the best of them. With the defense we had, it also made Tom's job that much easier. But he was truly the leader of the defense, a guy who got the job done for you."

Sestak himself was very proud of his team. In an interview conducted by this columnist a year before his death, Sestak remarked just how important the Bills' defensive unit was to their success.

"Without a strong defense, a team couldn't win a championship," remarked the late Sestak. "We had the defense. We accomplished what we set out to do.

"Probably the toughest teams we always had to play were the Kansas City Chiefs," commented Sestak. "They were such a big, physical team. I was big, at six-four, and I even had to look up at some of their guys.

"And there were several players who always gave me fits, including Ed Budde of the Chiefs and Charlie Long of the Boston Patriots. But in the end I never had an easy Sunday." Sestak always seemed to give a lot of credit to his teammates and none to himself. Sestak's former teammates agreed with that but knew differently and remembered Sestak in their own way.

"There were certain games that Tom dominated," said McDole. "He would explode off that line and go after a player. And the way our defense was set up, there were decoys used so that Tom and the rest of us could get to the quarterback or running back easier and faster. But usually Tom didn't need much help when it came to playing defense."

Dunaway agreed.

"Tom was one of the strongest players I've ever seen," added Dunaway. "He could overpower an offensive lineman without too much trouble. But what amazed me so much about Tom is that he played in such pain with his knees. He had bad knees, there was never a doubt about that. But it didn't stop him. He would be hobbling out there on the field and still make the plays. He made you play that much better. That's the kind of player Tom Sestak was."

Unfortunately, time and his painful knees caught up with Sestak. A five-time AFL All-Star and one of the most dominating defensive players in Bills history, Sestak announced his retirement from the game during the team's 1969 training camp. Sestak would later be named to the Bills All-Time Team during their 25th anniversary season.

Although Sestak is gone, he has never been forgotten. One thought that is remembered about the former defensive lineman is his philosophy about football. "Football is not a complicated game," Sestak would say. "I think coaches sometimes make it more complicated than it should be. Football is a game of tackling and blocking and just going out and hitting somebody. If you do that, you should be successful somewhere down the road."

Thomas Joseph Sestak, No. 70, was certainly all of that. And the mark he left on pro football will live on forever.

BOB KALSU

WHEN PEOPLE ENTER the ticket office entrance to Ralph Wilson Jr. Stadium, one of the first things they notice is the plaque on the wall to their right.

On it is an army helmet and a 1960s-style Buffalo Bills helmet. It is a tribute to former Bills tackle Bob Kalsu. Kalsu was one of the best tackles to ever play at the University of Oklahoma.

He was drafted in the eighth round of the NFL draft by the Bills in 1968. Kalsu played just one season for the Bills, 1968, before putting aside his promising pro football career in 1969 to serve in the United States Army in Vietnam.

On July 21, 1970, just 18 months after going into the army, Kalsu was killed by mortar fire while defending Ripcord Base on an isolated jungle mountaintop near Vietnam's Ashua Valley. He turned out to be the only NFL player, as well as professional athlete, to be killed in Vietnam.

While he may have played only one season in the NFL, the former guard with the Bills was remembered by his teammates. When Kalsu joined the Bills as a rookie for the 1968 AFL campaign, he was a backup.

Within a few weeks after joining the Bills, Kalsu was in the starting lineup. Veteran right guard Joe O'Donnell was injured at the time. Kalsu stepped in and replaced him.

"There was never a doubt in anyone's mind that Bob was a very good football player," recalled O'Donnell of the former All-America tackle. "He was a big boy [6'3", 250 pounds at the time]. And he seemed to fit right in. He was pushing all of the offensive linemen for their jobs, including Billy Shaw, our captain."

Shaw, who would later be elected to the pro football Hall of Fame in Canton, Ohio, in 1999, remembered Kalsu, who started eight games for the Bills in 1968.

"Bob came to the Bills as a very talented football player, as well as athlete," stated Shaw, who played for the Bills for nine seasons, 1961-69. "He was a tremendously strong player and was really good on the power sweeps. And, yes, I can remember the impression he made on me when he came to camp. He was a backup, not only for Joe, but for me as well. We didn't have as many players on the roster at that time like they do today. And Bob seemed to fit right in with the team. He had good speed and slipped right in there when we would go on a sweep with our running game.

"Of course, that one season he spent with us was one of our worst in the history of our franchise, injury-wise. That season we went through five different quarterbacks. We started the season with our regular starter, Jack Kemp. He got hurt and we went to Tom Flores.

"When Tom got hurt, we went to Dan Darragh. When Dan got hurt we had Kay Stephenson step in. Finally, when Kay went down, Ed Rutkowski finshed out the year for us. We finished the season with a 1-12-1 mark, dead last in the NFL," Shaw said.

"But through it all, Bob kept up with us. And that wasn't easy, having five different types of quarterbacks in the lineup throughout the season. But if there was one thing that always impressed me about Bob, it's how mature he was. He really didn't seem like a rookie that year with us. He never acted like one. He seemed like he always belonged. And the amazing part is that he had good football sense. You could show him something once, and he remembered it. He just never seemed in awe of anything. Bob just seemed comfortable with the surroundings."

A better person who felt that it was his duty to serve in the army full-time beginning in 1969. As fate would have it, Kalsu was killed in action.

Like many other Vietnam veterans, Kalsu's name is etched on the Vietnam Memorial Wall in Washington, D.C. And besides the plaque that hangs in the entrance at Ralph Wilson Jr. Stadium in Orchard Park, the Bills also honored Kalsu in 2000 when he was put on the Bills Wall of Fame.

"Bob Kalsu was a good person and football player," concluded Shaw. "But he will always be remembered as an American hero for the sacrifice he made for his country."

"Bob will always be a hero to all of us."

BOB CHANDLER

WHEN BOB CHANDLER SUDDENLY passed away from cancer, the news shocked family and friends alike. At 45, Chandler seemed to have a long life ahead of him to live.

"It's a shame, a real shame," said former Buffalo Bills offensive tackle Ken Jones. Jones played three seasons with Chandler when they were teammates with the Bills.

"Actually, it is a real tragedy. Here is a guy who kept himself in real good shape. He never smoked and ended up dying from lung cancer. It's just not right. Not right at all. He had so much to look forward to ahead of him."

Considered by many as one of the finest wide receivers to ever play in the National Football League, Chandler played 12 seasons of pro football. The Long Beach, California, native spent his first nine seasons of play with the Bills (1971-79). He concluded his NFL career with three seasons of play with the Oakland/Los Angeles Raiders, which included a Super Bowl championship in 1981 with Oakland.

Chandler was accorded several honors while playing college football at the University of Southern California. He was Player of the Game for the Trojans in the 1970 Rose Bowl win over Michigan. Chandler captained Southern Cal as a senior and also earned All-Pacific Eight honors as a flanker. He was also USC's pass reception leader in each of his three varsity seasons.

But in talking with other teammates of Chandler's, one found out that there was more to the former wide receiver than football statistics.

"Bobby was the classic person who got the most out of his athletic abilities," said former Bills linebacker, Shane Nelson, who played three football campaigns together on the Bills with Chandler.

"He played like he was six-four [Chandler was listed as 6' 1" and 180 pounds during his playing days]. Bobby always had to gain the respect from the coaches and other players on the opposing teams. He just didn't look like the wide receiver type. He was lean and lanky. But he was tough. Tough as nails. But he had character.

That character is what helped Chandler establish himself as one of the league's finest receivers. During a four-season period of time (1975-78) Chandler caught more passes (220) than any other player in the NFL. All of this despite knee problems and surgeries that may have slowed him down but didn't stop him.

"I think that's where the coaches took him for granted with the Bills," continued Nelson. "From a coaching standpoint, the Bills coaches always knew that hurt or not, Bobby would always be there every Sunday. You could count on him. I think the players knew how good Bobby was. They, too, also figured that Bobby would always be there to make the catch or block when it was needed."

Probably one player who knew Chandler as well as anybody was former Bills quarterback Joe Ferguson. Ferguson and Chandler played together with Buffalo for seven seasons.

"Bob was not your 'ra-ra' type of guy," recalled Ferguson. "He was a perfectionist. He got the most out of his athletic ability. But he went beyond that. Bobby played hurt. He played hurt a lot with the Bills. I know that a lot of people didn't know that, especially the fans and the media. Those of us on the team knew it. It just seemed like Bobby always gave more than he had to give. And he was a total team player. He would do anything for the team."

Evidence of that came during the famed 1973 season when O. J. Simpson gained over 2,000 yards in one season. The Bills were a run-oriented team, which meant just one thing for Chandler.

"Lou Saban [head coach of the Bills at the time] told Bobby very simply that either he would become a blocking wide receiver or he wouldn't play," remembered Ferguson. "So Bobby blocked and played a great deal that season.

"There really wasn't much else to do. I was a rookie quarterback that year. There wasn't much reason to pass when we had a runner like O.J. And believe me, Bobby was one of the best blockers I ever saw in football."

Ferguson also recalled a contest against the New England Patriots later in their careers when he threw a bullet that Chandler somehow managed to catch. To this day it is the one play that sticks out in Ferguson's mind to describe the kind of receiver Chandler was.

"Bobby ran across the back of the end zone," said Ferguson. "I saw him and just threw the ball as hard as I've ever thrown it. All I remember is that it went through two or three players before Bobby caught it and he ended up catching it behind him. He just

reached back and caught it. I don't know how he did it, but he caught it. But that was Bobby. You just knew where he was going to be. And he would always be in that spot. That was the confidence factor I had in Bobby Chandler as a wide receiver."

But there was also the off-the-field version of Chandler.

"Bobby was very quiet off the field," said Jones. "He really didn't say much. Not that he couldn't talk. It was just that he didn't go looking for conversations. But if somebody started talking to him, he could talk with the best of them."

Ferguson also remembered the off-the-gridiron Chandler.

"Bobby was well respected by his teammates as well as the public," stated Ferguson. "He was an individual. He didn't run with the crowd. But it should be understood that the Bills were a very close-knit team at that time. And Bobby was a part of that. It's just that Bobby had his own style. He was very mature. He did his own thing. He didn't let crowds bother him. Bobby handled people very well off the field."

Maybe Nelson summed it up best about Chandler.

"Bobby was class all the way. He handled himself well, both on and off the field. He gave everything he had both on and off the field. And he never asked for anything in return. Bobby Chandler was a good friend to many," Nelson said.

And he will be missed.

JOE DeLAMIELLEURE

JOE DeLAMIELLEURE LOVES football. He always has and always will. If DeLamielleure could have had his way, he would have played his entire 13 years in the NFL for nothing.

DeLamielleure, who was drafted by the Bills as the second pick in the first round of the 1973 NFL draft, remembers that first time he walked into the offices of the Bills.

"I walked into Harvey Johnson's office [Johnson was director of player development at the time for the Bills] with a pregnant wife, a '66 Ford with a dent in it parked in the parking lot, and no agent," remembered DeLamielleure. "That's right, no agent. I know that's unheard of today. But back then I just wanted to play football. I was the ninth of ten children and I was the only one in the family who had ever gone to college.

"For me, it was a privilege to play pro football. Coach Lou Saban made football fun. And what a first season I had. To say that the 1973 season was quite a season is an understatement. That was the year that O. J. Simpson broke Jim Brown's single-season rushing record with 2003 yards."

DeLamielleure was a big part of that record-breaking season. The Detroit, Michigan, native was a starter at guard and a very important part of the "Electric Company" line that led the way for Simpson to break Brown's record.

"The biggest thing I remember about that first season in Buffalo was the fact that I

OPPOSITE:
Joe DeLamielleure (right) and
Jim Ringo (left).

"The time I spent in Cleveland was nice. But it wasn't Buffalo. I felt that I never really belonged in Cleveland. Granted, I made another Pro Bowl team with them, but I really loved Buffalo, and so did my family.**"**

—JOE DeLAMIELLEURE

thought that this was the way things would always be in pro football," recalled DeLamielleure, who was an All-American at Michigan State. "It was easier for me than it ever had been in college. I remember driving to work every day and seeing all those guys in business suits driving to work and thinking what kind of jobs they must have. I saw the looks on their faces and how bored they looked. Me, I was happy going to the stadium every day to play football. And the thing that amazed me about all of this was that I was being paid to do it. This became real fun for me. Of course, little did I know that 2-12 seasons were lurking around the corner."

But DeLamielleure enjoyed his rookie season. He had to, especially with all the attention that he and the rest of his linemates were receiving thanks to Simpson.

"O. J. talked up the offensive line that year," remembered DeLamielleure. "He made the media and everyone else aware of us. He gave us a lot of credit for helping him break the rushing record. Combine that with television's instant replay, who were also focusing in on us now, and one could see why we were getting so much attention."

But the 1973 campaign would not be the only highlight of DeLamielleure's career.

Going to the Pro Bowl the first time ranks up there was well for the former Bills guard.

"I remember telling my wife during my rookie season that I would be a Pro Bowler by my third season," stated DeLamielleure. "As it turned out I was. I ended up going for five straight years. And you have to remember that I was being named to the Pro Bowl during some of Buffalo's worst years ever.

"For me, those were very frustrating years when the team was struggling. I wanted to see the team do well. But they just couldn't seem to get on track. And by the time they did, I was on my way to Cleveland."

Which was true. After being with the Bills for seven seasons, a five-time Pro Bowler at guard, DeLamielleure was traded to the Cleveland Browns.

"I never really wanted to leave," remembered the former guard. "But I just couldn't seem to get along with [Bills head coach] Chuck Knox at the time. And I ended up getting caught in the middle of a bad situation. There were other players who complained about Chuck to me. So I went with these complaints to Knox. Then we would go back to the players and try to resolve the problems, and some of the guys would deny ever saying anything. Nobody would admit to anything.

"It just made things between Knox and me that much tougher. So I ended up having to get out of Buffalo. I went to Mr. [Ralph] Wilson and asked him to please get me out of Buffalo. I didn't like Knox, but I didn't want to go public with it. So I was traded. The nice thing was that after Knox left, Mr. Wilson brought me back for one more season in Buffalo. I'll always appreciate that from him.

"The time I spent in Cleveland was nice. But it wasn't Buffalo. I felt that I never really belonged in Cleveland. Granted, I made another Pro Bowl team with them, but I really loved Buffalo, and so did my family. In fact, if we weren't living where we are today, my family and I would still be living in Buffalo."

DeLamielleure feels very fortunate to have been able to play pro football and get paid for it.

"I remember making $30,000 a year and thought I was stealing," commented DeLamielleure, who was elected to the Pro Football Hall of Fame in 2003. "I remember the first time a reporter asked me about the pressure of the game. I thought for a moment. Then I told him about my dad, who worked 19 hours a

Joe DeLamielleure (left)

day to make a living for our family. To me that was pressure. The only pressure in football is the pressure you put on yourself. To me, it's the greatest game ever played."

JOE FERGUSON

WHEN JOE FERGUSON WAS IN college he knew he had two choices for careers: a teacher or a professional football quarterback. Fortunately for the Bills and the NFL, Ferguson chose the latter.

"I knew that I would be making more money as a professional football player than teaching school," said Ferguson.

Ferguson played 18 seasons (1973-90) in the NFL with the Bills, Detroit Lions, Tampa Bay Buccaneers and Indianapolis Colts. But it was the first 12 seasons he spent in Buffalo that Ferguson is best remembered for.

In fact, the Alvin, Texas, native stepped right into the starting quarterback job in his rookie season with the Bills, starting all 14 games. But all of that got lost in the shuffle because of a running back by the name of O. J. Simpson, who had the

most memorable year a running back had ever had in the NFL up to that point in time. 1973 was the year that O. J. ran for an incredible 2,003 yards.

"It was unbelievable to have a guy like O. J. on the team," remembered Ferguson, who played his college football at the University of Arkansas. "He took a lot of pressure off of me. And I will admit that I learned a lot about football that year." But Ferguson will be the first person to also admit that he didn't realize the enormity of the record O. J. was chasing.

"Being the young, stupid guy that I was at the time, I never gave it [O. J.'s record] a whole lotta thought," stated Ferguson.

"About three-quarters of the way through the season I realized that he could do it [break Jim Brown's all-time one-season

> "And I knew that if I had a bad day, we would lose. If I had a good one, we usually won. When I made mistakes, the whole world seemed to be watching. It was very frustrating. In the end I was afraid to make a mistake."
>
> —JOE FERGUSON

rushing record]. I think most of us on the team really felt that final game of the season in New York when we played the Jets. The Bills had their PR people on the sidelines and they kept updating us on how close O. J. was getting to the record. I remember after O. J. broke the record I went over to the sidelines. I came back and told the guys in the huddle that O. J. only needed 60 yards to get 2,000 yards.

"I remember all of the guys getting real quiet and serious. It seemed like we all just tightened up a little more and said, 'Let's do it.' And we did."

But Ferguson recalled the darker side of Simpson's career with the Bills that took place in the mid-seventies. The season that turned everything sour was 1976.

"That was the year that O. J. held out for more money," said Ferguson, who was the Bills' third-round pick in the 1973 NFL draft. "Bills management kept saying there was no money. O. J. said that he would retire. As it turned out O. J. got his money and a lot of it. But he was the only guy on the team to get money of that kind. They gave all the money to one man. I think that affected and soured some of the players on the Bills team. It was after that the team seemed to come apart. Up

to that point, I thought we had a chance to really go places with the Bills."

The funny thing with the Bills in the post-O. J. era was that when things were going well, Ferguson got the credit. And when things didn't go well, he still got all the credit.

Things really got bad for Ferguson, so bad that it seemed like Buffalo fans were continuously booing him.

"It wasn't easy to accept the boos," remarked Ferguson. I worked hard, as did a lot of other guys on that team. We had an ordinary team after O. J. left. And we had some ordinary years. But I took the booing personally.

"And I knew that if I had a bad day, we would lose. If I had a good one, we usually won. When I made mistakes, the whole world seemed to be watching. It was very frustrating. In the end I was afraid to make a mistake. I knew that I didn't have the team to cover up the mistakes like I had earlier in my career. And the fans were at the mercy of the press. Things were written about me that just weren't true. And there was nothing I could do about it. Sometimes I was just glad to get out of town. It even got to the point where I wouldn't even watch TV or listen to the radio.

"Near the end of my career with Buffalo the press seemed to get on my physical ability. When we were winning I was fine. But when we lost I was considered 'over the hill.' That's why when I was traded [to Detroit] I was ready for a change. I felt it was time to move on and let somebody else take over. I had no regrets about leaving."

Much to the surprise of his critics, Ferguson lasted another six seasons in the NFL, mostly as a backup quarterback.

"I had prepared myself as I got older for my new role as a player," said Ferguson.

Ironically, by the time Ferguson left the Bills, he owned most of the team's passing records. Even more amazing was the fact that Ferguson never missed a start as quarterback of the Bills, which included 168 straight regular-season contests.

Probably one of the games that Ferguson is best remembered for occurred on January 3, 1981, in a playoff game in San Diego against the Chargers. Two weeks prior to that game Ferguson had hurt his left ankle against the New England Patriots. Playing courageously throughout the contest on a badly sprained ankle, Ferguson tried to direct a last-ditch effort to win the game for the Bills.

But by the second half of the game, Ferguson's ankle was hobbling him so much that the Bills offense couldn't get on track. They managed only 94 yards in that second half and lost the game, 20-14.

Ferguson left a lasting impression on many fans that day for his courage and leadership.

"We taped that ankle up as much as we could," said Ferguson. "But it really hurt. I just couldn't get going with it. When I got back home and had it examined a final time, it was discovered that the ankle had been sprained, torn, pulled and stretched. And there was a cracked bone in the back of my ankle to top it off.

"The tough part for me was that I knew that year was as good as our chances would ever get to winning. It was my big chance to get to the Super Bowl and it never happened." Not only did Ferguson never make it to the Super Bowl, he never made it to the Pro Bowl either. Despite that, there are some who believe that he is a viable candidate for the Professional Football Hall of Fame.

"I'd like to think of myself as a Hall of Fame candidate," responded Ferguson. "That would be quite an honor. But like everything else that's happened in my life, I just take things as they are dealt to me."

TONY GREENE

HOURS BEFORE THE BUFFALO Bills played the New Orleans Saints in an NFL preseason encounter, on a warm August afternoon in 1971, a young man was denied entrance into the Buffalo Bills player entrance to War Memorial Stadium. The denial had nothing to do with race, creed or sex.

"The guard at the door didn't think I looked like a football player," recalled former Bills safety Tony Greene, who was only 5' 10" and weighed less than 170 pounds at the time.

"One of the Bills trainers came out and told the guy who I was. He said he was sorry and I got in."

Greene would never be denied entrance to a professional football stadium again, although throughout Greene's nine-year career with the Bills (1971-79) there were

opponents who would have liked to lock him out of their stadiums.

Once inside the confines of War Memorial Stadium, Greene wondered if he was in the right place.

"I went out onto the field for the pregame warmups, and I couldn't believe what I saw," recalled Greene, a native of Bethesda, Maryland. "The stadium was so old looking. The locker rooms were in terrible shape, too. I just couldn't believe that they would allow something like this to take place in the National Football League. I couldn't believe that this was a pro stadium in the National Football League."

Greene also recalled what fellow teammate John Pitts told him prior to the start of his first pro game.

"He told me to keep my helmet on at all times," said Greene. "He told me not to take it off. But it was a very warm night and it was getting hot, so I took it off, despite John's warnings. The minute I took it off, oranges, cans and other garbage came flying towards me. I immediately put my helmet back on and never took it off again, no matter how hot it got."

Actually, Greene was just pleased to be playing in the NFL. A defensive back and onetime captain for the University of Maryland's football team, Greene had not been selected in the 1971 NFL draft. Although he was disappointed, Greene felt that he should be given a chance to prove his abilities.

The Bills gave him that chance, signing him as a free agent in 1971. And thanks to an assistant coach they had on the team at the time, Greene signed with Buffalo.

"Ralph Hawkins [an assistant coach with the Bills from 1969-71 and 1981-82] had been a coach at Maryland when I was there," remembered Greene. "He was one of the main reasons I signed with Buffalo. I could have signed with several teams, including the Dallas Cowboys or Washington Redskins, two teams who had also contacted me, but I just felt as though I had a better chance of making it with the Bills. It just happened that I was in the right place at the right time."

During his nine seasons with Buffalo, Greene had many memorable moments including earning All-Pro honors in 1974 (despite missing the final two games of the regular season because of a knee injury), playing in the Pro Bowl after the 1977 campaign, and being named defensive captain of the Bills from 1974-76.

Greene also holds the Buffalo record for the longest interception return, 101 yards, against the Kansas City Chiefs on October 3, 1976.

"Again, it was just a case of being in the right place at the right time," stated Greene. "All I remember is that I caught the ball and just took off with it. A few key blocks were thrown and I was on my way. But actually, that wasn't as big as the one I had called back against the Miami Dolphins in Miami [back in 1974]. That one was for 105 yards. And it wasn't as easy to make it to the end zone in that one as it had been against the Chiefs. Unfortunately, it was called back because of a penalty.

"All I remember about it was that it was an awful long walk back to the other end of the Orange Bowl in that heat."

Greene didn't hesitate when naming some of the top opponents he faced during his NFL career.

"As for quarterbacks, it would have to be Bob Griese [Miami], Ken Stabler [Oakland Raiders] and Ken Anderson [Cincinnati Bengals]," stated Greene. "I would also put Jim Plunkett [New England Patriots and Raiders] up there as well, especially for his toughness. He was one tough guy. As for receivers, there was Paul Warfield [Miami], Reggie Rucker [Cleveland Browns], and Cliff Branch [Oakland]. Branch was the fastest guy I ever had to face. I thought I was fast when I came into the league, but the first time I faced Cliff, I knew better. And as for running backs, the two that stick out above the rest in my mind were Larry Csonka [Miami] and Earl Campbell [Houston Oilers]. These were two very big individuals. And there was nothing worse than facing either one of them with a full head of steam going. You just knew that you were in for the hit of your life when they ran into you."

The two teammates that stick out in Greene's mind the most are Jim Braxton and Bob Chandler, both of whom have passed away. Braxton was a huge running back, who blocked for O. J. Simpson during his glory days, and Chandler was a wide receiver.

"The three of us were very close and were like the three musketeers," remembered Greene. "I roomed with both of those guys. We learned a lot about each other. We talked a lot with each other. We were close. We had a very special relationship. They were a big part of my life and now they're gone and I'm the only one left of the three. I miss them." Another player Greene misses is Simpson, who was arrested for murder but later acquitted.

"I faxed him a letter soon after he was arrested," added Greene. "I really feel bad for O. J. But I believe that we must let the justice system do what's right."

Mentioning Simpson also brought back memories of that magic 1973 season when O. J. broke Jim Brown's single-season record for most yards gained with 2003. While Greene admits that the spotlight was on O. J., the defense wasn't doing all that bad, either.

"I always thought we had a pretty good defense," stated Greene, the club's MVP in 1974. "We had guys like Earl Edwards, Mike Kadish, Walt Patulski, Jim Cheyunski, John Skorupan, Robert James and myself. We were pretty good, especially as we got closer to Brown's record. I can especially remember that final game against the Jets in New York when O. J. was close. All the defense kept talking about that day was getting the ball back from the Jets offense so our offense could get back on the field. And it worked. It was nice to be a part of that record and NFL history."

Greene never played in a Super Bowl, although he feels the closest the team ever came was in 1974.

"I have always felt that with one play here or there, we could have gone on to the Super Bowl that year," said Greene. "Although there was nothing that was going to stop the Steelers from going all the way that year, I think we still had a good team."

Greene was named the recipient of the Ralph C. Wilson Jr. Distinguished Service Award. The award was established in 1986 to honor former Bills players for long and meritorious service.

"It came as a total surprise," commented Greene about the award. "Usually after a player leaves a team, they don't get recognized again, especially after you leave the city you were playing in. This is a wonderful award, and I'm very pleased to be receiving it. I still follow football," concluded Greene, who finished his career with 37 interceptions. "I would like to get back into the game in some kind of front-office capacity. I know I might have to pay some dues. But that's how I made it as a player and that was worth it."

ROBERT JAMES

ALL ROBERT JAMES EVER wanted out of pro football was a chance to play. The Buffalo Bills gave the former cornerback that chance in the summer of 1969.

James went on to make the Bills and play for six seasons in the National Football League before a devastating knee injury ended his playing days in August 1975. During that short period of time the Murfreesboro native became an inspirational team leader for Buffalo and earned the respect of opposing teams for his tight-pass defensive style of play and jarring open-field tackles.

The former cornerback was never forgotten in Western New York, and in 1998 was named the 13th inductee on the Bills' Wall of Fame. His name was placed on the Wall just below the video scoreboard. He joined 12 other honorees, including O. J. Simpson,

Jack Kemp, Pat McGroder, Tom Sestak, Billy Shaw, Ralph C. Wilson Jr., the 12th Man—the Bills Fans, Mike Stratton, Joe Ferguson, Marv Levy, Joe DeLamielleure and Elbert Dubenion.

It was Dubenion, scouting for the Bills at the time, who discovered the honored cornerback. James had come out of tiny Fisk University in Murfreesboro, Tennessee, in '69. He was an undrafted free agent who played defensive end and linebacker in college.

"It had been my dream to play pro football," recalled James. "I had confidence in my ability. But I knew that I didn't come out of a big name college. Then 'Duby' came along. He had been traveling through Nashville. He told me that the Bills were looking for quality ballplayers.

"At the same time the Bills were looking at me, so were the Dallas Cowboys and Pittsburgh Steelers. The Cowboys' interest in me faded quickly. But the Steelers' didn't. The only difference was that Duby brought along a contract for me to sign. I was desperate so I signed right away with Buffalo. Ironically, the Steelers came along a week later, but they were too late. I was on my way to Buffalo."

The Bills had come off one of their worst seasons in franchise history, finishing dead last in the NFL with a 1-12-1 record. They relieved their interim coach, Harvey Johnson, and replaced him with John Rauch, who had left the Oakland Raiders to come to Buffalo.

For their efforts in 1968, Buffalo drafted Simpson number one out of the University of Southern California.

"Buffalo had high expectations for O. J.," remembered James. "But I knew that he couldn't turn their entire program around in just one year. I also think that people expected a lot out of Coach Rauch. He had come from the Raiders, where he had helped develop a winning organization. I found out very quickly that the people in Buffalo were used to winning and wanted a winner right away."

James recalled his first two days of training camp, especially day two.

"My first day I really struggled," admitted James. "I had the speed, but I couldn't backpedal very well that first day. I wasn't sure I was going to make it past day two until I found out that the team was going to have a scrimmage. In that scrimmage we were allowed to hit. I knew I could hit and I did. I hit hard. By the end of day two I had earned the respect of both the coaches and the veteran players. That turned things around for me, and I was on my way."

James also talked about the conversion from linebacker to cornerback.

"It was a natural move for me," added James. "I had all that untapped speed that Duby knew about. I had run the 40-yard dash in college in 4.4. I didn't think that football scouts would make a big deal out of that. I was simply running a 4.4."

The only thing that James couldn't adjust to was losing, something the Bills continued to do during his first four seasons in the NFL. Buffalo again hit bottom in 1971 when they finished dead last in the league again with a 1-13 mark. He also admitted that playing in War Memorial Stadium took some getting used to.

"When I got to Buffalo, I guess I expected more," said James. "I'll have to admit that War Memorial Stadium wasn't what I was used to. But I was glad to be in Buffalo and playing pro football.

"But I never got over the losing. I wasn't used to that, and it was something I didn't want to get in a habit of doing. But that all changed when Lou Saban arrived."

Saban came to Buffalo for his second stint in 1972. Although he didn't produce a winning team that first year (the Bills finished 4-9-1), there was a different attitude on the team.

"We had drafted some new players on the team, traded for some others, and things began to turn around," stated James. "I knew that it wasn't the coach alone that would make a football team a winner. You need good players."

By 1973 the Bills were on their way with a winning record. While O. J. was making the headlines with his running exploits, it was James and the rest of the Bills defense that made the team complete. By 1974 the defense was limiting opponents to 17.5 points per game while picking off 20 passes.

Following four knee surgeries and one attempted comeback, James retired and returned to Murfreesboro, where he became a teacher and school administrator.

"My plan had been to play 15 or 16 years in the NFL," remarked James. "I would have played the game for nothing if that's what they had wanted me to do. I was at the top of my game when I got hurt. I really felt comfortable. I had perfected the art of playing cornerback. But it just wasn't in God's plan for me to play more. Instead, he's given me a chance to work with children.

"My plan had been to play 15 or 16 years in the NFL. I would have played the game for nothing if that's what they had wanted me to do. I was at the top of my game when I got hurt. I really felt comfortable. I had perfected the art of playing cornerback. But it just wasn't in God's plan for me to play more. Instead, he's given me a chance to work with children."

—ROBERT JAMES

Buffalo made the playoffs that year for the first time in seven years. James was on a roll, being named to three straight AFC-NFC Pro Bowl Games (1972-74).

Things were looking great for James and the Bills in 1975. Then disaster struck. During a preseason game against the Los Angeles Rams at Rich Stadium, James intercepted a pass from former Buffalo quarterback James Harris. While running back the interception, James was tackled by the Rams' Lawrence McCutcheon. McCutcheon's shoulder slammed into James's knee. James career was finished.

"And now to receive this honor from the Bills, I am deeply grateful. The Bills are a first-class organization. As a walk-on, they gave me a chance to play. They have a good relationship with their players. They have a quality of excellence in their organization.

"I've been very blessed. I've dealt with the options that life has dealt me. I've accepted them and just moved on. That's what we all have to do."

REGGIE McKENZIE

DURING HIS COLLEGE DAYS at the University of Michigan, Reggie McKenzie was taught by coach Bo Schembechler to always set goals for himself. It was instilled in McKenzie that nothing was impossible to attain.

McKenzie went on to prove to the world that he was a good student of Schembechler's, especially in 1973. It was during the summer of that year that the former guard set a goal for the Bills running back, O. J. Simpson, that everyone thought was unattainable: to gain 2,000 yards rushing in one NFL regular season.

To go along with high-range goals, McKenzie was a proven winner.

"Coming out of Michigan with Coach Schembechler, I played with teams that recorded a 32-4 mark," recalled McKenzie, who played in the NFL as an offensive guard with the Bills and Seattle Seahawks from 1972 to 1984. "We just didn't lose. And I wasn't used to losing after I got to the Bills."

McKenzie was a member of the 1970 and 1972 Michigan Rose Bowl teams and was a two-time All-Big Ten selection. In his senior year he was a consensus All-American. Drafted by Buffalo as a second-round selection in 1972, the 27th player taken in the NFL draft that year, McKenzie was coming to a team that had gone through five consecutive losing campaigns, including a 1-13 mark in 1971. McKenzie's rookie season wasn't much better, as the Bills marched through a 4-9-1 season.

Although McKenzie wasn't happy with the campaign, he was amazed by something else that had occurred that year.

"I remember coming to Buffalo that year and seeing O. J. gain a thousand yards for the first time in his NFL career," remembered McKenzie, a native of Detroit, Michigan. "I just couldn't believe that. I knew that he could do better. A lot better. I couldn't believe that my first year with the Bills was his first that he had gained over a thousand yards. That was O. J.'s fourth year in the league. And I knew, as a team, that we could do better. Much better."

With that in mind, McKenzie went ahead and proposed the idea of the 2,000-yard season for Simpson in 1973. Although it seemed like an impossible goal to attain for many observers, including the great O. J. himself, McKenzie felt the team could to it.

"O. J. will be the first one to tell you that he didn't think it was possible," stated McKenzie. "He was still doubting that he could break the record early in the [1973] season. It wasn't until the seventh game of the season against the Kansas City Chiefs on *Monday Night Football* did O. J. believe that he could go for 2,000 yards."

As the record shows, by the time the Bills defeated the Chiefs that night, Simpson had over 1,000 yards for the season. Now 2,000 seemed an attainable goal.

"Our confidence was at an all-time high," said McKenzie of the Bills. "We were winning and everything seemed to be going our way. I just figured that there would be nothing standing in our way to get O. J. the record."

McKenzie remembered Buffalo's second to last game of that season against the New England Patriots.

"We crushed New England in that game, just like we had in our opener that year," commented McKenzie. "In fact, I thought O. J. could have easily gained over 300 yards in that second game against the Patriots. Unfortunately, it snowed, and there was two inches of snow on the ground for O. J. to run on. So it made running a little difficult for him, as well as all of us that day. But I'm still convinced that had it been a nicer day, O. J. could have broken 300 yards and had the 2,000-yard mark for the year that day. Instead, we had to wait a week and set the record in New York against the Jets."

McKenzie also recalled Simpson, the overall player.

"O. J. was a tough sucker, too," stated McKenzie. "He didn't let injuries get in the way of his playing ability. A lot of people don't know how many times O. J. fought through injuries and continued to play. To me, that was just one of the factors that separated O. J. from other running backs."

McKenzie, like many others at the time, felt that the Bills were just a player or two away from a Super Bowl. But it was not to be.

"We needed a little bit of help on the defense at the time," stated McKenzie. "Offensively, teams just couldn't stop us. We were a very tight group. When we ran plays, we all knew where each player was supposed to be. It was like clockwork.

"And we didn't let anybody touch O. J. or Joe Ferguson. They were the guys who were the stars. If you messed with them, you had to go through the rest of the offense first."

As it turned out, McKenzie never made it to a Super Bowl, at least as a player. After 11 seasons with the Bills, McKenzie spent his final two years in the NFL with the Seahawks before retiring from the game in 1985.

McKenzie's record with the Bills speaks for itself. He was a fixture in the starting lineup from his rookie season on. He had 140 consecutive starts. That ended when

he suffered a knee injury that put him on injured reserve for the final eight games of the 1981 campaign.

McKenzie earned UPI second-team All-AFC honors in 1980 after being elected to several All-Pro and All-Conference teams in 1973 and 1974.

"I still follow the Bills today," said McKenzie at the turn of the 21st century. "I'm very proud of the accomplishments they have had over the past few years. I still feel like I'm a member of the Bills. I believe that once you're a Bill, you're always a Bill."

LOU SABAN

AFTER JUST TWO SEASONS WITH the Buffalo Bills, Buster Ramsey was fired on January 4, 1962. Just 14 days later, Lou Saban was hired as the team's new head coach, signing a one-year deal worth approximately $20,000. It would be one of the many stops Saban would make in his coaching career. In fact, Saban would have two stints with the Bills, the first from 1962-65 and the second from 1972-76.

Bills owner Ralph Wilson had hired Saban as the team's director of player personnel just six weeks into the 1961 AFL campaign. Saban had been released just a couple of weeks earlier as head coach of the Boston Patriots.

Actually, there isn't a level of football that Saban hadn't coached at, including high school, small college, major college, AFL, NFL, USFL, WFL, and Arena. But it's the

Bills teams from the 1960s that held a special place in Saban's heart, especially the AFL championship team of 1964.

"I have a great fondness for that '64 club because I had a total trust in them as a unit and as a group of young people," Saban told the Rochester (N.Y.) *Democrat and Chronicle.* "It was a great romance. In all my years of coaching—and I've had some fine teams—I remember this as one of the top teams I'll ever have the privilege of coaching."

Saban's most memorable game and moment with the Bills came on December 26, 1964 in the AFL championship game between Buffalo and the San Diego Chargers at War Memorial Stadium. It occurred when Bills linebacker Mike Stratton hit Chargers running back Keith Lincoln, breaking four of his ribs and knocking him out of the contest.

" I was simply just a coach who had a plan of attack. I was only as successful as the players would perform. "

—LOU SABAN

It was the turning point in Buffalo's 20-7 victory over San Diego and winning their first AFL title.

"That tackle kind of put the emphasis on what we planned to do," said Saban, who was named AFL Coach of the Year in 1964 and 1965. "We were a rough-and-tumble group, we were great tacklers, great defensive people and we loved to play tough when things were tough. After that play, I could see it unwind. I could see that we were going to become the champions of the American Football League."

The Bills would go on to win another AFL championship in 1965 under the guidance of Saban. But in a surprise move, Saban resigned as head coach of the Bills on January 2, 1966 to take the head coaching job at the University of Maryland. He would later return to Buffalo to coach the Bills again and rejuvenate O. J. Simpson's football career.

Following an awful 1971 football season, Saban returned as head of the Bills in 1972. He guided Buffalo into the 1974 NFL playoffs. He remained as head coach in Buffalo until October 15, 1976, when he suddenly resigned. He left Buffalo with a career record of 70-47-4 and a winning percentage of .600, second only to Marv Levy.

"There is no doubt in my mind that Lou is the guy who turned O. J.'s career around," recalled Bills cornerback Robert James.

"Prior to Lou's arrival back in Buffalo, O. J. had struggled with his running game.

"But after Lou came, he centered the Bills' offensive attack around O. J."

Saban knew that he had to win with Simpson in the lineup.

"I think this was a Bills team that had won just 13 games in the previous five seasons before I came back," recalled Saban. "I knew that I couldn't wait to build a team from scratch. We needed to start winning. And O. J. was the logical player to build around. I knew the enormous talent that he had as a running back. He wasn't the same type of punishing runner I had back in '64 with Cookie Gilchrist. O. J. had a bit more flair to his running game.

"I just felt that if I could get O. J. going, the rest of the offense would follow."

And it did. Just two seasons after his return, the Bills were playoff contenders again.

"I simply had a plan, and O. J. and the rest of the players put it in motion," concluded Saban, who passed away at the age of 87 in 2009. "I was simply just a coach who had a plan of attack. I was only as successful as the players would perform."

As the record shows, somehow they always performed for Saban.

O. J. SIMPSON

BEFORE THE 1973 NFL season, football teams' offensive lines were virtually unknown entities. But that was before O. J. Simpson and "The Electric Company" came along.

Nineteen seventy-three marked the first time in the history of the NFL that a running back gained more than 2,000 yards rushing during the regular season. O. J. was the type of player who wouldn't take all the credit alone. He knew that if it hadn't been for his offensive line blocking for him, not only would he have never come close to breaking Jim Brown's all-time mark of single-season rushing total of 1,863 yards, but he would have never even thought about 2,000 yards.

The nickname for the offensive line came from the Bills' director of public relations, L. Budd Thalman. Everybody with the Bills referred to Simpson as "Juice," short for his college nickname, "Orange Juice." So why not name the line "The Electric Company" because "they turn loose the Juice"?

"The Electric Company" was made up of centers Bruce Jarvis and Mike Montler, tackles Dave Foley and Donnie Green, guards Joe DeLamielleure and Reggie McKenzie, and tight end Paul Seymour.

During his days at the University of Michigan, Reggie McKenzie had been taught by coach Bo Schembechler to always set goals for himself. It was instilled in McKenzie that nothing was impossible to attain.

It was during the summer of 1973 that the former Bills guard set the goal for Simpson. Many thought McKenzie had flipped. Even Simpson himself thought it was impossible.

"It was just something I thought was tough to attain," recalled Simpson, the Bills' as well as the NFL's number-one pick in 1969. "I had a lot of respect for Jim Brown and what he had accomplished. I thought we could come close, but 2,000 I thought was a big goal to shoot for."

"O. J. will be the first one to tell you that he didn't think it was possible," added McKenzie.

"He was still doubting that he could break the record early in the (1973) season. It wasn't until the seventh game of the season against the Kansas City Chiefs on Monday Night Football did O. J. believe that he could go for 2,000 yards. In fact, a week before the KC game, O. J. felt that he had a shot at 1,000 yards in just seven games. And I remember Juice coming to me and saying the week of our Monday night game, 'I've got a present for Howard [Cosell, commentator for *Monday Night Football]*. A thousand in seven. That's what I'm going to give my buddy Howard.' And O. J. went out and did it against KC."

Simpson says he wasn't thinking about the record—until the end of the Bills' first game that season.

"I never really thought about 2,000 yards. I wanted to lead the league in rushing. I wanted to be the best at running back. You always wanted to be the best at whatever you do. That year I ran for 2,000 yards, I never expected it to happen. The Bills were a team that had had five or six losing seasons in a row. We just wanted to turn things around in Buffalo and start winning," Simpson said.

"It was after our opening game at home against the Boston Patriots when I gained 250 yards rushing in a single game that we started talking about 2,000 yards. In fact it was my main man, Reggie McKenzie, who told me after that game to forget about the rushing record. Forget about a thousand yards. Let's go for 2,000 yards. I didn't think that it was possible. But I liked his enthusiasm. I don't think there was ever a group of guys as close as we were on our offensive unit. We accomplished that record as a unit. If it wasn't for them, I wouldn't have made it.

"We knew, going into that last game against the New York Jets, that we were going to break Jim Brown's all-time mark and that we were going to get the 2,000 yards. It didn't matter how many times I would have to carry the ball. We were going to break that mark. It didn't matter if it was snowing or not in that last game in New York. We went on that field very enthusiastically," Simpson recalled.

DeLamielleure was a rookie in 1973 for the Bills. It was quite an introduction, to say the least, for the guard from Michigan State.

"The biggest thing I remember about that first season in Buffalo was the fact that I thought that this would be the way things would always be in pro football," recalled DeLamielleure.

"It was easier for me than it ever had been in college. And who wouldn't have enjoyed that 1973 campaign? After all, how many other offensive lines had ever received the attention that Joe D. and his mates were receiving thanks to Simpson?"

89

O. J. SIMPSON

"O. J. got **250 yards** that day to set a single-game rushing mark, and I knew then that this was going to be **a special year. "**

—BILLS CENTER BRUCE JARVIS

Jarvis was Buffalo's starting center for the 1973 season. A player with excellent size and good pass-blocking abilities, Jarvis would play only half the campaign, missing most of the second half with a knee injury. The University of Washington center remembered the magic season.

"I think to this day that we were struck by the success we had," said Jarvis. "The Bills had been a losing franchise. Things had not been going well. One thing that people forget is that we had a new stadium that year. We had over 80,000 fans coming each week to watch us.

"Because of that we were enjoying a tremendous upsurge in fan appreciation. I believe that really made a difference for us. I give a lot of credit to the success of the franchise that year to the fans. They really made a difference. You have to admit that we were a better team at home than on the road.

"And the players really appreciated the fans and their support. It really got us into games."

Jarvis knew the kind of season it was going to be in just the first game against the New England Patriots.

"O. J. got 250 yards that day to set a single-game rushing mark, and I knew then that

this was going to be a special year," continued Jarvis. "I remember O. J. heading out on a long run. It was one of those plays that seemed to run the way it was designed to run. It was 'picture run.' You knew right then that we would have a great season. I didn't realize that it would be one for 2,000 yards. But you knew it would be special."

Jarvis recalled the preseason and what many experts were saying about the Bills.

"We were a young, inexperienced team," he commented. "Veteran Irv Goode had come over in a trade, and he was supposed to solidify the offensive line. But a rookie like Joe D. turned out to be a little better at the position that expected. When we opened the season we had all six spots hitting—working together very smoothly. Everything seemed to fall into place. We had all six blockers in place. Plus, we had great wide receivers like J. D. Hill and Bob Chandler who sacrificed themselves and would block. They were two of the best blocking wide receivers I've ever played with or against. And we had Jim Braxton exploding out of the backfield. He could really block. Joe Ferguson didn't make many mistakes as a rookie quarterback either. Our coaching staff brought a conservative approach to our offensive game. The opposition really wasn't expecting us to do much. But as many found out, we were still running over people in the second half of the season as much as we were in the first half."

Unfortunately for Jarvis, he was in a hospital room recuperating from knee surgery when Simpson broke the 2,000-yard mark at Shea Stadium against the New York Jets. Taking his place was Montler, a veteran offensive lineman, who had never played center until coming to the Bills in 1973.

"The coaching staff felt that I could handle the position," commented Montler. "Offensive line coach Jim Ringo [a former center] really put a lot of faith in me in that position. Ringo never asked any of us to do something he really felt that we couldn't handle. We played to our strengths."

Montler also felt that the coaching staff seemed to be very flexible.

"O. J. was always paying attention to what was going on during the game," said Montler. "He would make some suggestions about our game plan. Lou [Saban] was very flexible when it came to things like that."

The former center also recalled the final two games of the year when 2,000 yards seemed out of reach because of circumstances beyond the team's control.

"The final two games seemed to be played in some pretty bad weather conditions," stated Montler. "But O. J. went out in both games and got the yardage. In fact, when we got to New York it was snowing and the field was really in poor condition by the second half."

Montler admits even to having a strange thought or two about that final half when O. J. broke the record.

"I remember sitting in the locker room thinking of what official would throw a flag in that second half," he said. "After all, could you imagine on the play that O. J. got the 2,000 yards, a flag being thrown against Buffalo? Call the play back? Hardly. We just went out there in that second half with a great deal of determination and tried to blow the Jets right off the field."

For Foley, who had been cut from the Jets two seasons before, it was almost a prefect sweet revenge when Simpson broke the rushing record.

"That was a very special moment for me, not only because I was playing in a part of NFL history, but that it happened against the team that had gotten rid of me a couple of years before," remembered Foley.

But even Foley admitted that he would have never bet on O. J.'s gaining 2,000 yards in a single season when training camp opened.

"It seemed like the coaching staff was trying out players all the time during that period of time," said Foley. "For certain players, the circumstances were really great for opportunities to play for the Bills. That's why I have to give a lot of credit for our line's success to Jim Ringo. He was great. He really knew the talent on this team, and especially on the offensive line. And it really helped to have a runner like O. J. in your backfield. He is one of the greatest runners I have ever seen play the game. He is one of the greatest of all time."

Foley pointed out the fact that there was one special player on their line.

"Paul Seymour was our tight end, but he was more like a blocking guard for us," stated Foley. "We were very fortunate to have a player like Paul blocking on our line. And he wasn't a bad receiver, either."

Cosell once referred to Seymour as the "World's Biggest Tight End." Seymour was also a rookie on that 1973 Bills team. Like his linemates, Seymour remembered the special attention paid to "The Electric Company."

"Our offensive line won the 'Outstanding Lineman of the Year' award from the NFL,"

remarked Seymour. "I think it was the only time that an entire offensive line was honored like that. But then again, nobody ever had an offensive line like the one the Bills had that year."

Like others before him, Seymour was quick to give credit to his offensive line coach, and described Ringo and what he was like as a coach.

"He was a fiercely quiet kind of guy," he said. "He was so quiet that there were times that we, as players, couldn't even hear him. But he could take apart another team's defense. He capitalized on our strengths. He was a very good instructor. And he didn't put pressure on any of the guys to perform.

"As the team's number-one draft choice that year, he just told me that certain people might expect a lot of me. But that was all. Not even Lou Saban ever mentioned that I was a number-one pick. I was just another guy who had a job to do on the football team."

Seymour also recalled that famous game at Shea Stadium on December 16.

"We felt coming into that game that O. J. would break Jimmy Brown's all-time single-season rushing mark and that he would break the 2,000-yard mark," commented the former tight end. "I know I never

doubted it for a moment. If the field conditions got bad, then things might have gotten tough for O. J. But they didn't, and we went out and broke all kinds of records. But that's just the type of line we were. We had so much confidence. We always felt that we could blow any defensive line away if we wanted to. And we did that year."

Green seemed to look at things a little differently than others.

"I remember watching that last can of film of the Jets on a Friday," said McKenzie. "We knew that day that we were going to get it. When you, as a group like we were, begin thinking you can accomplish something like this, you can do it. They just couldn't stop us.

I remember the moment O. J. broke Brown's record. After a little celebration, we got back into the huddle and I said something like, 'OK, now let's go for the 2,000.' It was that simple.

> "We were a **very close-knit offensive line** both on and off the field. We did a lot of things together. And it seemed like **every time O. J. got a hundred yards** in a game, we felt the same way. That's how close we were."
>
> —BILLS TACKLE DONNIE GREEN

"It was a fun season that year O. J. broke the records," stated Green. "We all had fun on the field that year. And the other part was that we all played as one unit. We were a very close-knit offensive line both on and off the field. We did a lot of things together. And it seemed like every time O. J. got a hundred yards in a game, we felt the same way. That's how close we were. Of course, I had never seen a running back like O. J. in my life. It was a blessing to be on a team with O. J. And off the field he was a genuine person. A good person. Always seemed to have time for kids."

McKenzie recalled the final steps leading up to the great record-breaking moment as if it were yesterday.

"But you could see it in the eyes of the rest of the guys that nothing was going to stop us from our mission. We knew the PR people were on the sidelines telling us how close O. J. was getting to the mark. Finally we did it, and what a moment. What a moment!"

Seymour may have summed things up the best.

"We set our sights on a goal and we made it," concluded Seymour. "We had a good group of guys to do it. We got along well and believed in each other. That was the magic of our success. And O. J. too. He was one of the greatest runners to ever play in the NFL."

JERRY BUTLER

PROBABLY EVERY WIDE receiver who has ever played in the NFL has dreamed of making his last catch a great one. A touchdown.

That is how Buffalo Bills wide receiver Jerry Butler ended his career. Unfortunately, he wasn't ready to end his career at the time. It was just before the end of the first half against the Miami Dolphins in Buffalo, November 16, 1986. Butler had just caught a 25-yard touchdown pass from quarterback Jim Kelly.

As the Bills receiver came down with the ball, two Miami defenders came down with him, right on top of his leg. Butler knew the minute he hit the Rich Stadium turf that something was wrong.

"I knew it was bad," recalled Butler. "As it ended up, I had a compound fracture of the ankle, tore ligaments in my ankle and broke my leg. "Now I had come back from serious injuries before. But as it turned out, this is one that I wouldn't come back from."

Butler played for the Bills for eight seasons, although one (1984) was spent on the injured reserve list. He was the Bills' second pick in the first round of the 1979 NFL draft (Tom Cousineau was the first), and was the fifth player chosen overall.

Butler had come a long way from his days in his native Greenwood, S.C. The former wide receiver grew up in that small town never really dreaming of an NFL career. He never started playing organized football until his sophomore year in high school. In fact, he went to college at Clemson on a track scholarship.

"But the coaches there gave me the opportunity to participate in both track and football," remembered Butler. "I had never really thought about playing football in college. But I did. And before I knew it, I was in the pros."

Butler's career with the Bills seemed to be filled with adversity. It seemed that every time he turned around he was suffering from some type of injury, no matter how big or small it may have been.

"I separated my shoulder in my rookie year," recalled Butler, who missed three games because of that injury but still managed to grab 48 passes for 834 yards and won AFC Rookie of the Year honors.

"I even had an operation on my eye. Probably the worst injury I suffered before my career-ending one came in 1983 when I hurt my knee. I not only missed the rest of the 1983 season, but all of the 1984 one as well. I injured my knee when I caught my toe on the turf at Rich Stadium in a game against the New Orleans Saints. It was terrible."

"I took the following year off and kept on rehabilitating the knee. By 1985 I had worked my way back into the starting lineup. I just never gave up hope."

Never giving up seemed to be Butler's theme as a receiver as well. At least it seemed that way every time a football was thrown his way.

"My high as a football player came from trying to catch anything, and my main goal in pro football was to be a great receiver. I took great pride in trying to catch everything that was thrown close to me. I was very tough on myself."

Butler had the opportunity to play with two outstanding quarterbacks, Joe Ferguson and Jim Kelly.

"Both guys were very similar as quarterback," stated Butler. "Both could really throw the ball when they had to. But both guys had very strong leadership qualities that were very important to the team."

One of Butler's more memorable games as a receiver occurred in his rookie campaign against the New York Jets on September 23, 1979. In that game Butler made 10 receptions for 255 yards and four touchdowns. It was a remarkable feat, to say the least.

"It was just one of those games that everything that seemed to come near me, I caught," remembered Butler. "I just couldn't do anything wrong that day."

Butler looks back on his NFL career with great pride. But he often wonders "what if" when he thinks about the injuries he suffered during his career.

"I took great pride in my work. But I had to overcome a lot of adversity throughout most of my career," said Butler. "I always figured that I could overcome anything after coming back from my first serious injury in 1983. I missed the entire 1984 season working my way back into the lineup.

"That's why when I got hurt the second time in 1986, I figured that I would come back from that was well. But I just kept running into problems. I finally realized after talking with four different doctors that I wasn't going to come back from this one. I think it would have been interesting to see how I would have still fit in with that team."

Very interesting.

JIM RITCHER

JIM RITCHER ADMITS THAT he was never able to catch up.

Catch up? To what?

"The size of guys playing in this game," answered Ritcher. "When I came into the league back in 1980, I weighed around 238 pounds. I thought that was pretty big for an offensive lineman. But not in the NFL.

"When I came in some of the heaviest guys in the league weighed 270 pounds. So I decided that I would work on building myself up to that standard. By the time I got to my 13th season, I weighed a little over 270 pounds. And guess what? The heaviest guys in the league that I went up against weighed over 300 pounds. I just couldn't seem to catch up. Of course, I didn't really want to continue to put on the extra weight at that point of my career."

Ritcher played 14 seasons in the NFL, all with the Bills. That broke the team record for consecutive seasons played, formerly held by quarterback Joe Ferguson and defensive back Steve Freeman.

Ritcher was a first-round draft pick of Buffalo in the 1980 NFL draft (the 16th player taken overall). Despite all of those record-breaking performances and longevity, Ritcher wasn't recognized for his outstanding play as a Pro Bowler until his 12th season of play. That was truly amazing, considering all of the hoopla that followed Ritcher when he arrived in Buffalo in 1980.

The Berea, Ohio, native came out of North Carolina State University as one of the most honored college players in the country. He was the 1979 Outland Trophy winner as the nation's top lineman, only the second offensive lineman to win it. Ritcher was also a two-time consensus All-American.

But when he arrived in Buffalo, things didn't go exactly the way Ritcher had planned.

"That first year with the Bills was certainly a frustrating one for me," commented Ritcher.

"Being a first-round draft pick, a lot was expected of me. Coming into college I had been a defensive end. Then I was a center in college. Becoming a guard in the pros was quite an adjustment. I was basically a backup my first year, and I played quite a bit on the special teams. But it was still quite frustrating.

"The man I have to give a lot of credit to during those early years of my pro career is Chuck Knox. When Chuck was coaching the Bills, he really took his time with me and let me develop on my own. He didn't rush me. He was very patient with me all the way through my early days. He didn't panic. I'll always be grateful to him for that."

Another individual whom Ritcher credits with helping him during the early part of his career is his former Bills linemate Joe Devlin.

"He supported me in everything I did," said Ritcher. "Joe took me under his wing and taught me a lot of things that, as a veteran player, he really didn't have to do. He taught me the Bills system at the time. He worked with me. Most of all he believed in me when many others didn't."

Following three seasons of preparation, Ritcher was ready for a starting role as a left guard for the 1983 season. He never relinquished the spot after that. He admits that he changed quite a bit after those early days with the Bills. After a few years he didn't practice with a mouthful of worms or eat wine glasses and beer mugs.

"Yeah, I guess I really did those things when I first came to Buffalo," recalled Ritcher. "Don't ask me why. I guess you might have called me young and foolish."

Ritcher also credits being healthy over those 14 seasons as a major reason for accomplishing the records he did with the Bills. But that has also resulted in another necessary attitude adjustment for the big offensive lineman.

"When I was younger, I never really worried about injuries," stated Ritcher. "I always felt early in my career that if you got hurt, you could always come back from it. I never really gave injuries much thought. Near the end of my career I did. Then I worried if I got a bad injury, I wouldn't come back from it as quickly. I was very fortunate in my career not to have had any serious injuries. I had surgery, but nothing that really stopped me from playing."

And Ritcher admits that he was glad to play his entire career with the Bills.

"Again, back when I was young and foolish, I never gave thought about being traded," said Ritcher. "But I soon realized that trades were a part of the game. I really like Buffalo. It's a great city and a great area to raise a family. I became involved in the community and felt very comfortable there.

"The Bills fans put up with a lot over the years, both winning and losing, the good times with the bad. I was really glad to be a part of those Super Bowl teams."

And Ritcher stated that he knew when it was time to retire.

"When the good Lord told me it was time to go and do something else, I knew it was time," said Ritcher. "I read things. I listened to those around me. I just knew when it was time and that was it."

Jim Ritcher (left).

FRED SMERLAS

WHEN THE BUFFALO BILLS drafted Fred Smerlas in the second round of the 1979 NFL Draft, they knew just exactly what they were getting.

"We had a guy coming to the Bills that we knew would never quit on us," said former Bills head coach Chuck Knox. "Norm Pollom [the Bills' chief scout at the time] had told me that he had never seen a player like Fred before.

"You have to remember that Fred came from a college team [Boston College] that had not won a game in his senior year [1978, BC went 0–11]. Yet the scouts that saw Fred play all had the same report. And that was that despite how bad his team might be losing in the fourth quarter, Fred would still be coming on with every play. With that kind of

play on such a poor team, we knew that we had a guy that wouldn't give up on anything when we got him."

Fred Smerlas played for the Bills for 11 seasons (1979-89) and was the cornerstone of the Buffalo defense during the 1980s. Smerlas was a five-time Pro Bowler with the Bills during his career, which saw him play 162 games for Buffalo and record 29.5 sacks in that time.

Smerlas played backup to Mike Kadish his first season. After that he was the team's nose tackle for good. Smerlas played 155 games in a row, a streak that is second in team history behind Darryl Talley's 204-game streak.

OPPOSITE:
Fred Smerlas (76).

Wide receiver Jerry Butler joined the Bills the same year that Smerlas did. He was always impressed with Smerlas as a player and a person.

and Ben Williams in the early 1980s and Bruce Smith, Shane Conlan and Cornelius Bennett in the late 1980s were able to make great plays.

"Fred was one of those **hard-nosed type** players who sacrificed himself for other guys. He could tie up guys on defense to open us up and make the big plays. He was **a key factor in the success** our defense had during that period of time."

—DEFENSIVE TEAMMATE BEN WILLIAMS

"You had to be a little unique to play that nose tackle position," recalled Butler. "You have to remember that a guy in that position is going to get hit by two or three players on every play.

You have to have some mental toughness to be able to take that game after game and play after play.

"But Fred also had a great sense of humor as well. He had something to say about everything. You just never knew what was going to come out of his mouth. And he could make you laugh, or at least smile, with some of the things he said. And I don't think anybody ever scared him out on the field. He was always ready for any challenge thrown his way."

In the early 1980s Smerlas, along with inside linebackers Jim Haslett and Shane Nelson, formed the famed Bermuda Triangle defense. Because Smerlas could tie up two or three players on each play, fellow defensive teammates like Haslett, Nelson

"Fred was one of those hard-nosed type players who sacrificed himself for other guys," remembered Williams. "He could tie up guys on defense to open us up and make the big plays. He was a key factor in the success our defense had during that period of time."

Smerlas, who was chosen for the Bills Wall of Fame in 2001, knew what his job was and what it took to play it.

"I know that you have to be a little crazy to play this position of nose tackle," commented Smerlas. "I never worried about the money I made when I went out on the field to play the game. I was always focused on one thing when I went out on the field, and that was to play football. The game was the only thing on my mind. For me, football has always been an obsession. My life has revolved around football and it always will. When I played, I never cared what I looked like. Every game was the same. I needed a shave, my shirt was out, there was blood all over the front of it, and I didn't care how much mud was on me. The more mud there was the better. I looked ugly and I played ugly. Period.

"As for my sense of humor, that's something I've always had. I had to have a sense of humor to play the position I played."

Former Bills quarterback Joe Ferguson, who was a teammate of Smerlas's for six seasons, recalled the nose tackle's style of play.

"He was a guy who could keep a team loose if they needed that," stated Ferguson. "He had a great sense of humor. But Fred was serious when it came to football. He was all football. He always seemed at the center of everything on defense. He didn't always get credit for the sacks or tackles. But he created enough havoc out there to free up other players on the defensive line or at linebacker for us. And he didn't keep quiet on the field either. He was always talking to offensive linemen lining up across from him. He would do anything to get an edge. And he would do anything to upset the opposition. He was perfect for his position."

Maybe the first paragraph of Smerlas's book, *By A Nose,* written with writer Vic Carucci, sums up the nose tackle's career.

"I make a living as a nose tackle," wrote Smerlas. "This should tell you right away there are a few loose toys in my attic. No one in his right mind would spend more than a single play there. I've been in my wrong mind for 11 years. There isn't another player in league history who has spent more time at the position. I guess that makes me a nose for the ages."

JIM KELLY

TIME.

Former Buffalo Bills head coach Marv Levy once said that "time has a way of healing old wounds."

Time was certainly on former Bills quarterback Jim Kelly's side. When Kelly retired following the 1996 NFL season, he held nearly every major passing record in Bills history. He had also established himself as one of the greatest quarterbacks in league history.

The next step in Kelly's storied career would come five years later when he would become eligible for election to the Pro Football Hall of Fame in Canton, Ohio. There were some football experts at the time who felt that Kelly might not be elected on the first ballot. While he was considered one of the great quarterbacks of the game, he had also lost four Super Bowls in a row from 1991-94.

Kelly is Buffalo's all-time leader in pass attempts, completions, completion percentage, yards, touchdown passes and 300-yard games. When he retired, Kelly was ranked sixth in NFL history in passer rating, eighth in completions, tenth in yards, twelfth in touchdown passes and thirteenth in attempts.

Yet those four Super Bowl losses still hung over Kelly's head.

But five years later, Kelly not only was elected to the Hall, but was chosen in his first year of eligibility. So what happened over those five years? The four Super Bowl losses in a row didn't disappear.

"I really think time has a lot to do with it," stated Larry Felser, retired football writer and columnist for the *Buffalo News*. "It took five years, but a lot of people connected with

football are beginning to realize just what Kelly and the Bills really accomplished. John Madden, Don Shula and Archie Manning all agree that an NFL team will never appear in four straight Super Bowls again. They just believe that it will never be done again.

"Add to that what Kelly did statistically, and everything just came together for him when it came time for election to the Hall. It's just the fact that people are just beginning to appreciate Kelly for what he did, especially those four Super Bowl appearances in a row."

Felser also believes that Kelly was the key to the great years of the Bills from the late 1980s through the mid-1990s.

"There is no doubt that Jim was the main engine in the resurgence of the Bills in the late 1980s," continued Felser. "When Kelly joined the Bills in 1986, you just knew that things were going to turn around for the Bills."

The Bills were just coming off the darkest era in their history, back-to-back 2-14 seasons in 1984 and 1985. Kelly had been a first-round draft choice of Buffalo in 1983. But instead of signing with the Bills, Kelly opted to ink a deal with the Houston Gamblers of the United States Football League. When the USFL folded in 1986, it didn't take long for the Bills to get Kelly signed.

"What Jim did for the Bills and Buffalo— he just raised the city," recalled Bills owner Ralph Wilson Jr.

And he won.

"He bumped heads with some of the best quarterbacks the game has ever seen," added Felser. "He went head to head with the Marinos, Elways and Montanas. He had a better winning record than all of them. I've always considered Joe Montana, Otto Graham and Johnny Unitas as the three greatest of all time as quarterbacks. Kelly would be in the next level of quarterbacks. To me, Bobby Layne would be in the same category as Kelly."

Most would agree that is good company.

One of Kelly's teammates from that era of football greatness with the Bills is center Kent Hull. Like Felser, Hull agrees about the effect time has had on Kelly doubters.

"As years pass, what we accomplished as a team with four straight Super Bowls and all, I appreciate it more and more," commented Hull. "I think that the rest of the country has swung around to that thinking as well. When you see what's happening with free agency and the cap system, the chances of a team going to four straight Super Bowls is becoming slimmer and slimmer. Actually, I don't think it will ever be done again."

Hull explained what it took to make the Bills one of the most successful NFL franchises of the 1990s.

"A good head coach surrounds himself with good assistants, which is just what Marv did with the Bills," said Hull. "And a good quarterback surrounds himself with good talent. Kelly certainly had himself surrounded with good talent. He had a good line in front of him, as well as a good running game and great receivers. And I think that's what separated the Bills from other teams of that era. For example, the Dolphins had Marino and that was it. They really didn't have a running game. But if Jim couldn't get the passing game going, he could go to Thurman Thomas and the running game."

Hull was with Kelly right from the start with the Bills.

"Fans were expecting a lot out of Jim when he arrived in Buffalo in 1986," continued Hull. "When Jim joined the team they had instant credibility. And by his third season on the team the Bills had won the AFC East. And by that fifth year, the Bills were on their way to the Super Bowl."

While Hull will be the first to admit that there were several leaders on the Bills during the 1990s, there was only one leader when it came time to talking first in the locker room.

"When we would have a team meeting, Jim would always be the first one to speak. It was just what would happen."

Another teammate, Steve Tasker, agrees with Felser and Hull when it comes to Kelly's election to the Hall.

"As the years have worn on, people began to focus on just what Jim did, versus what the Bills didn't do," stated Tasker. "The main thing Jim did was that he taught the Bills how to win. Jim was one of the all-time great quarterbacks. He was still one of the top quarterbacks in the NFL when he retired. The problem Jim had at that time was the fact that people were comparing him to himself. The problem was that Jim didn't have the same supporting cast surrounding him that he did at the beginning of his career.

"Jim did most of his leading on the field," recalled Tasker. "But he was a leader off the field as well. Jim was a good chemistry professor. He really made an effort to keep good chemistry on the Bills. He did this by inviting his teammates and their families to his home for parties and get-togethers. Jim was the ultimate when it came to creating the extended family. He was a good teammate, but he took it to another level when he brought in their families. He was a very unique leader for the Bills. It comes as no surprise that he went into the Hall. We'll just have to wait and see how many of his teammates will follow him in. And time will once again play a role in that, because only time will tell."

As time has told, several of Kelly's teammates followed him into the Hall. They included Thurman Thomas, Bruce Smith, James Lofton and Andre Reed. Original owner Ralph Wilson as well as head coach Marv Levy also joined Kelly in the Hall.

Although Kelly retired from the Bills following the 1996 NFL campaign, he remains the face, as well as the heart and soul of the Buffalo franchise. The former quarterback also devoted a great deal of his time to his son Hunter James Kelly.

Hunter was diagnosed with Krabbe disease at the time of his birth in 1997. His father established a non-profit organization called Hunter's Hope the same year to help increase awareness of the disease.

Unfortunately, Hunter lost his battle with Krabbe in 2005.

But Kelly's battles were not over with. In 2013 he was diagnosed with squamous cell carcinoma, a form of cancer, in his jaw. After battling it for over a year, it was announced that Kelly was cancer-free in late August of 2014.

But three months later the former Bills quarterback announced that receiving an eight-week treatment for a methicillin-resistant Staphylococcus aureus (MRSA) infection.

"Kelly Tough," as the phrase is known about Kelly and his family throughout Western New York, is once again the situation the former Bills quarterback finds himself in.

"We're all pulling for him again," said Tasker. "We all hope for the best."

KENT HULL

KENT HULL REMEMBERED the day back in May, 2002, when Buffalo Bills owner Ralph Wilson called him on the phone.

"I was gone at the time," recalled Hull, the former center for the Bills for 11 seasons, 1986-96. "Mr. Wilson had left two messages for me. I really thought he wanted me to coach. In fact, that's what I was all set to talk about when I finally did talk to him. That's when he told me that I was going up on the wall."

Hull is referring to becoming the 19th person, 14th player and fourth offensive lineman to be added to the Bills Wall of Fame. The former center, who anchored the line for the Bills' famed no-huddle offense, was taken by surprise with the honor.

"I just can't believe that something like this would ever happen to me," remarked the 41-year-old Hull. "I must admit that I was stunned, to say the least, the day that Mr. Wilson called me. This is the greatest honor that has ever been bestowed on me. I'm really looking forward to coming back to Buffalo."

And in turn, Bills fans in Buffalo got one more chance to celebrate the heart and soul of the Bills' offensive line of the late 1980s and early 1990s.

"I was thinking about what to say to those fans," said Hull. "They are the greatest fans in the world. If it wouldn't have been for them, I probably would have retired earlier in my career than I did."

Former teammates realize what Hull met to the team and its fans.

"Kent is one of the most popular players to ever wear a Bills uniform," commented former teammate Steve Tasker. "A guy like Kent

"He was one of the guys who really helped hold the team together. He was a leader in the truest sense of the word."

—SPECIAL TEAMS PLAYER STEVE TASKER

was a guy that fans, as well as the rest of us, sometimes took for granted. He was always there, game after game. For 11 seasons he was one of the guys you could count on to help run our offense. I know that Jim [Kelly] trusted and depended on Kent a lot, especially when he was running the no-huddle offense. They worked very well together."

Interestingly enough, Hull began his football career as a quarterback at Greenwood High School in Mississippi. But in his senior year he switched to center because of a growth spurt he had.

Following four years as a center at Mississippi State, Hull was drafted by the USFL's New Jersey Generals in 1983. Surprisingly, he was not drafted at all by the NFL. Hull became one of the USFL's top players. It didn't come as any surprise when the Bills signed him in 1986. As history shows us, Hull signed his Bills contract the day after Kelly signed his.

The former center missed only two games in his 11 seasons in a Bills uniform, playing in 121 straight games before missing two starts. He then resumed another streak, playing 68 straight starts before retiring.

Hull recalled those early years with the Bills.

"The team had hit bottom and had no place to go but up," remembered Hull. "We were starting to put together the nucleus of the team that would eventually go to four straight Super Bowls. But the two most interesting years occurred in 1988 and 1989. Nineteen eighty-eight was a breakout year for us and the year we learned how to win together. But 1989 was the year that we learned how to lose together. I think we learned a lot from that year. Remember, the next year we came back and won again and this time we went to the Super Bowl for the first time.

"The Bills really started becoming confident in what we could do. Confidence became a big part of this team. And we weren't cocky or arrogant. It was confidence. You could see it in the big games we played in over the years."

And like many of his teammates during that Bills era of football, Hull had very strong feelings about those teams that went to four Super Bowls in a row.

"As years have passed, I appreciate more what we accomplished," said Hull, who received the Ralph C. Wilson Jr. Distinguished Service Award in 2001 along with Tasker. "I think the rest of the country has swung around to that thinking. I just don't think you're ever going to see a team go to the Super Bowl that many times in a row again."

Tasker believes that Hull was a key player in that success.

"He was one of the guys who really helped hold the team together," remarked Tasker. "He was a leader in the truest sense of the word."

Hull had another way of saying that.

"I would like to be remembered that I was a teacher and a diplomat," added Hull.

"I always seemed to be in the middle of all the little fights that took place on the team. All I ever wanted to do is just fit in and play football. I never expected to last as long as I did with the Bills. In fact, I never even thought I would make it past that first season. After I got past that first one, I just kept taking it one year at a time. It was one great ride, one which will never be duplicated. And I'm glad I was a part of it."

Sadly, Hull left this world too early. On October 18, 2011, Hull died from a chronic liver disease, a condition he had been suffering from for several years.

"Although Kent is gone, he will never be forgotten by those of us who were his teammates," concluded Tasker. "He was a true teammate."

MARV LEVY

"HE WAS JUST THE RIGHT GUY for the right job." That is how Buffalo Bills linebacker Darryl Talley described Marv Levy. Levy coached the Bills for all or parts of 12 seasons (1986-97). At the time Levy joined Buffalo, the Bills had suffered through two consecutive 2-14 seasons under two head coaches, Kay Stephenson and Hank Bullough.

Following a Bills loss on November 2, 1986, Bullough was fired and Levy took over. Many thought at the time that because of his age, 60, Levy would be just a short-term head coach who would help get the team and organization turned around.

After all, this was something Levy had done before. He had joined the Kansas City Chiefs in 1978 and coached them for five seasons. When he joined the Chiefs, they were coming off a disastrous 2-12 campaign.

In his first season in KC, the Chiefs finished 4-12. By 1979 the team concluded with a 7-9 campaign. By Levy's third season, Kansas City was 9-7.

At the time Levy took over the Bills, they were 2-6. In his first game on the sidelines for Buffalo against the Pittsburgh Steelers, the Bills came away victorious, 16-12. Although the Bills finished the season 2-5 under Levy's leadership, he came back the following year to continue the rebuilding process.

The rest, as they say, is history.

"When I joined the team, we had the nucleus of what would eventually become a Super Bowl team," recalled Levy. "We had Jim Kelly at quarterback and Andre Reed at wide receiver. There was Bruce Smith and Darryl Talley on defense.

General manager Bill Polian was building toward a championship team. I would become fortunate enough to be the person put in charge of running the club on the field."

Talley recalled that Levy seemed to have the right chemistry at the time that the players on the team were looking for.

"Things had not been good under Hank Bullough," remembered Talley. "The attitude on the team was not a good one. We were a team that was spinning out of control. I think those of us on the team at the time who would end up going to four Super Bowls with Marv as coach felt that a change was needed. Jim Kelly was very frustrated at quarterback. He was a winner who just seemed to be going nowhere under Hank.

"It was all different when Marv entered the picture. Things seemed to change right away. True, we didn't win a lot of games under him that first season. But our attitude changed. He ran practices differently. He was very organized. He instilled a positive and winning attitude in us. And as we would find out in later years, Marv Levy was the right guy because he knew how to handle each and every one of us on the team. He knew which buttons to push at the right time and he would do it."

The 1987 season was a forgettable one for the Bills as well as the rest of the National Football League. The season was marred by a strike, which lasted three games. Buffalo finished with a 7-8 mark. But by the 1988 campaign, Levy was in control, and the Bills were ready to take off. They finished the season with a 12-4 record, winning the AFC East. They beat the Houston Oilers in the AFC Divisional playoff contest, 17-10, before losing to the Cincinnati Bengals, 21-10, in the AFC championship contest.

"It was like daylight and dark when Marv took over from Hank Bullough," stated Steve Tasker, a special teams player at the time, who would play 12 seasons for the Bills and all but eight games under the leadership of Levy." Marv brought a calmness to the team.

"Marv also brought in an attitude of believing in yourself. I think he turned out to be more than just a head coach for most of us that played for him at the time with the Bills. I think everyone liked Marv. But more importantly, I think everyone who ever played for Marv Levy respected him as a person and head coach. He always seemed well organized, had a good game plan and kept the team focused. And most importantly, he never gave up on the team. He instilled a positive attitude with us. He treated us like men, like people and not just players."

By the time Levy retired from his coaching position with the Bills following the 1997 season, he had left his mark on Buffalo, as well as the NFL. He was the only coach in league history to lead his team to four consecutive Super Bowl appearances. His 154 coaching victories placed him 10th on the all-time NFL list. His 123 wins as a Bills coach are a team record. In 11 full campaigns as coach in Buffalo, he led his team to eight postseason appearances.

Levy's 11 postseason victories tied him for fifth place on the NFL's all-time list. And Levy tied an NFL record in his final season when he coached the Bills at age 72, tying him with the legendary George Halas of the Chicago Bears as the eldest coach in league history.

His favorite saying with the Bills during his coaching tenure, which he would say before each kickoff, was, "Where would you rather be than right here, right now?" Everyone knew the answer to that question when Levy was elected to the Pro Football Hall of Fame in 2001, and he made the Bills Wall of Fame in 1996.

"I was proud and honored to coach the Bills," said Levy at the time of his retirement announcement. "I had many great thrills over the years I coached the Bills. But one of the proudest moments for me came in 1992 when we beat the Houston Oilers in the AFC wild card game.

"As everyone knows, the game is known to all as the greatest comeback in NFL history [the final score was 41-38 in OT]. I think that showed everyone the type of team and character the Bills had at that time. Simply put, our guys never gave up in that game."

Tasker put it another way.

"It was a game that was typical of a Marv Levy–coached Buffalo Bills team," concluded Tasker. "We knew the odds were against us going into the second half of that game. All we needed was a break, and we got it. We just never gave up. And Marv wouldn't let us give up. He always believed in us, and we believed in him and ourselves. It was a great winning combination."

"Marv also brought in an attitude of believing in yourself. I think he turned out to be more than just a head coach for most of us that played for him at the time with the Bills. I think everyone liked Marv. But more importantly, I think everyone who ever played for Marv Levy respected him as a person and head coach. He instilled a positive attitude with us. He treated us like men, like people and not just players."

—SPECIAL TEAMS PLAYER STEVE TASKER

ANDRE REED

THE GAME IS SIMPLY CALLED "the Greatest Comeback Ever."

For Buffalo Bills wide receiver Andre Reed, it may have been one of the finest games he ever played. It was Reed who caught three straight touchdown passes to give Buffalo a 38-35 lead in the closing minutes of regulation time.

In one of the most unbelievable games ever played in NFL history, the Bills rallied from a 35-3 deficit to beat the Houston Oilers, 41-38 in overtime, in an AFC wild-card playoff game at Buffalo's Rich Stadium.

What makes the game even more amazing for the Bills is that they were missing starters Jim Kelly (QB) and Cornelius Bennett (LB), who did not dress for the game because of injuries, as well as Thurman Thomas (RB) who missed the second half of the contest

with a hip pointer. "It was just a case of believing in each other," said Reed. "We had faith in the people who were in the game replacing those guys who were injured, especially quarterback Frank Reich. But if you'd have asked me at the moment we were down by 28-3, I would have told you that it didn't really look great for us. It actually looked kind of hopeless. It was just a case of our defense not being able to stop their offense. It just seemed like the Oilers offense was going up and down the field at will and we weren't able to stop them.

"But then something happened to the Oilers. I'm not sure what. They made a couple of mistakes that we took advantage of, and we were back in the game."

OPPOSITE:
Andre Reed (83) hauls in a pass.

One other little-known fact is that the 79 points the two teams scored tied for the most in an NFL playoff game, matching the amount scored by the San Diego Chargers and Miami Dolphins in their 1981 contest, which also went into overtime.

After building up a 28-3 halftime lead, the Oilers seemed on the verge of really putting the Bills away in the third quarter. On just the third play of the quarter, Reich threw an interception that Houston's Bubba McDowell ran back for 58 yards and a TD. At that point, with the Oilers leading 35-3, the game seemed to be all but over. Reich, who had engineered college's greatest comeback when he was at the University of Maryland (down 31-0 at the time) knew that he and the Bills had their work cut out for them.

"Your thought is to take it one play at a time and don't force anything," said Reich. Which is exactly what he did.

After the Oilers scored, the Bills went on a 10-play drive, capped off by a one-yard run by Kenneth Davis, in for the injured Thomas, for a TD to make the score 35-10. Following the recovery of an onside kick, the Bills went four plays. The final one saw Reich connect with receiver Don Beebe for a 38-yard scoring play. That made it 35-17. Houston had to punt again on its next possession. The Bills took over. Reich hit James Lofton for 18, followed by a Davis run of 19. Reich then hit Andre Reed for a TD, making it 35-24.

Before Houston knew it, the Bills had the football again, thanks to a Henry Jones interception of a Warren Moon pass. Reich eventually faced a fourth-and-five situation for the Bills. After calling a timeout, Reich threw a TD pass to Reed to make it 35-31 with two minutes left in the third quarter.

The Oilers could have finally put some more points on the scoreboard early in the fourth, but they muffed a field-goal attempt and the Bills took over. Seven plays and 74 yards later, Reich again found Reed again in the end zone for a TD. With 3:08 left, the Bills led, 38-35.

The Oilers tied it on an Al Del Greco field goal. Houston also won the toss in OT, but on just third play of the OT, Nate Odomes intercepted Moon and the Bills took over at the Houston 35. After running several plays, Buffalo's kicker, Steve Christie, nailed a 32-yard field goal to win it.

"Without question, it's the game of my life," said Reich. "I was pretty emotional when I got back to the locker room, I couldn't hold the tears back. I never really thought, 'Oh, we're out of it.' I still had to go out there. When we scored to make it 35-24 late in the third quarter, that's when I thought it was really within reach."

For Reed, who today holds most of the Bills' receiving records, it was very special to him to have played such an important role in such a monumental game.

"It is part of our legacy as a team during that era," said Reed. "I feel that game was the type of game that I was becoming known for. I've always said that I wanted to be remembered as the guy that, when the chips were down, could be called upon to make the big play. And when I was called on, I did make the big play. And I think I showed that in the greatest comeback ever game."

Reed's efforts paid off following his retirement. The former wide receiver became eligible for induction into the Pro Football Hall of Fame in 2006. While other wide receivers of his era went into the Hall, Reed continued to fall short on the percentage of votes needed to enter.

Reed was finally elected to Pro Football's Hall of Fame in 2014. His selection solidified Reed's place in pro football history.

"There was never a doubt that Andre belonged there," said former Bills head coach, Marv Levy, also a member of the Hall. "He showed that during his days with the Bills.

"Game in and game out, Andre was always there for us. He was one of those players you could count on in key situations.

"He proved he belonged in the Hall and now he is there."

BRUCE SMITH

"IT'S HAMMER TIME."

Those words were all the Buffalo Bills defense needed to hear when defensive end Bruce Smith was on the field. When they heard Smith utter those words, everyone knew Smith was ready to lead the Buffalo charge on defense.

"It was a defensive thing," remembered Smith, now in his 19th season of play in the NFL and presently playing for the Washington Redskins. "It was considered big plays on defense. It was just doing something big to disrupt the offense. And we would pound on the opposition's offense until they couldn't take it anymore. And then you would pound some more. That was what would make me happy. If I could disrupt something on the other team's offensive approach to the game, then I had done my job. I've really felt that the Bills, especially during our Super Bowl years of 1990-93,

we were one of the most punishing teams defensively in the entire NFL.

"We would pound you starting on the offensive line. We pounded the running backs and quarterbacks. And we would punish the wide receivers. When you played the Bills, you knew that you were in for a rough, physical game. It was just like driving a nail into wood with a hammer. You just keep pounding the nail into the wood until you can't see it anymore. And then you pound some more."

Smith was the anchor on the Bills' defensive line for 15 seasons, from 1985 through 1999. Other members of the defense during that era of four straight Super Bowl appearances included the front line of Smith, Phil Hansen, Leon Seals, Jeff Wright, linebackers Cornelius Bennett, Mark Maddox, Shane Conlan, Ray Bentley, Marvcus Patton, Carlton Bailey and Darryl Talley and defensive backs Kirby

Jackson, Nate Odomes, Leonard Smith, Dwight Drane, James Williams, Henry Jones, Mickey Washington and Mark Kelso.

"Bruce was the guy who made the defense go," said Talley. "He could physically do things that I had never seen a defensive lineman do before. I've seen him double-teamed by an offensive line and still be able to get to a quarterback or running back. There may have been other guys who were as quick as Bruce. But as strong? I don't think so."

early in his career when he was with the New England Patriots.

"When we faced the Bills, there was always one thing I would tell our offensive linemen in front of me and that was to somehow take care of Bruce Smith," recalled Bledsoe. "For a big guy, he was very agile. I was always watching out for him when he came off the line.

"When Bruce and the Bills were on their game, I didn't have much time to think

"Bruce is one of the **most dominating defensive players** in the history of the NFL. He just seemed to be all **over the field** when he was playing."

—BILLS SPECIAL TEAMS PLAYER STEVE TASKER

During his 15 seasons with Buffalo, Smith was a Pro Bowler 11 times and a two-time NFL defensive player of the year.

"Bruce is one of the most dominating defensive players in the history of the NFL," remarked Bills special teams player Steve Tasker. "He just seemed to be all over the field when he was playing.

"He could hit you as hard as anyone. He could run as fast as anyone. He could come off that defensive line as quick as anyone. I saw him blow by guys on an offensive line before they knew what hit them. And he was so confident in his ability. He knew what he could do and how good he was at doing it. Was it arrogance? I wouldn't say so. I would say it was more confidence than anything. I would have to say that Bruce is one of the greatest defensive linemen of all time."

Quarterback Drew Bledsoe, now with the Bills, remembers facing Smith many times

back there in the pocket with Bruce running around. And when he hit you, you knew it. And it just seemed when he was on his game, there was nothing you could do to stop Bruce Smith. I know that I faced Bruce during the prime of his career and at the end of the Bills' Super Bowl run. But he was still great," Bledsoe said.

"I know that there have been a lot of great defensive ends out there over the years. Reggie White was another great one. But in my estimation, there was nobody quite like Bruce Smith. Maybe it's because I used to face him at least twice a season. And believe me, sometimes that was two times too many."

Hansen believed that Smith made everyone better on the Bills defense.

"There was never a doubt in my mind about that," said Hansen. "Because of his play, he could draw a lot of attention to himself. That opened up a lot of opportunities for other guys on the line and at linebacker. And if that happened, then teams would try and take care of that. When that happened, it would open things up for Bruce again. It was a great winning combination. He created a lot of havoc out on the field. He was an emotional player who could lead by example.

"To me, Bruce Smith will always be considered the best at his position."

Following his career with the Bills, Smith went on and played four more seasons with the Washington Redskins. At the time of his retirement following the 2003 NFL campaign, Smith was the League's all-time sack leader with 200. He is the only player to reach the 200 mark.

History proved that statement when Smith was enshrined into the Pro Football Hall of Fame in 2009, along with Bills owner and founder, Ralph Wilson Jr.

"It was a great honor to go into the Hall with the man who was responsible for the Bills existence," said Smith, who is also a member of the Virginia Sports Hall of Fame, College Football Hall of Fame and the Buffalo Bills Wall of Fame. "This is a very high point in my life, but a very humbling one as well to be included with all of these other NFL greats."

Maybe Hall of Fame offensive tackle Anthony Muñoz summed it up the best when the former Cincinnati Bengal was asked what it was like to go up against Smith. His single-word serious statement said it all.

"Scary."

DARRYL TALLEY

DARRYL TALLEY'S MOST MEM-orable moment as a football player didn't come during a game. It actually came during a pregame.

"It was during the national anthem of Super Bowl XXV," recalled Talley, an outside linebacker with the Buffalo Bills from 1983-94. "It was in our very first Super Bowl and we were all trying to focus on the game. I remember hearing the anthem and then seeing those planes fly overhead. It really gave me the chills. What a feeling it was."

Talley played a total of 14 seasons in the National Football League (1983-96), his final two campaigns with the Atlanta Falcons and Minnesota Vikings. But it was his time with Buffalo that established him as one of the most complete linebackers to ever wear a Bills uniform.

During his time in Buffalo Talley played in 204 straight games, including postseason, a record that may never be broken.

"Darryl was one of those players who gave it his all, all the time," recalled former teammate Steve Tasker. "I guess it became a situation of almost taking Darryl for granted.

"He was always there in the lineup. I didn't realize until his career was over with how many games he had played in a Buffalo uniform. I know that he must have played through a lot of games in pain. When I look back on it, there was nobody tougher than Darryl Talley. They might have been as tough, but nobody was tougher. That's what made him so good."

Another teammate, center Kent Hull, remembered Talley quite well.

"Darryl was a kind of wild man back at that linebacking position," said Hull. "There were some days when he just seemed to be all over the field and was in on almost every defensive play. And when he hit guys, man they knew that they had been hit. He could really ring bells. All I know is that I'm glad that I didn't have to play against him."

Another thing Talley is remembered for is the fact that he came out of the same draft that Bills quarterback Jim Kelly did. Drafted in the second round of the 1983 NFL draft, the 39th player taken overall, Talley came to Buffalo from the University of West Virginia.

"It was a real struggle those first three seasons I was in Buffalo," remembered Talley. "We just didn't seem to have any organization. And then Marv Levy came to town. I've never met a better man. And I believe to this day that he was the only guy who could have ever coached this team. Marv always made you think. And he always said that he had only two rules. The first was don't be dumb. The second was don't be dirty. That was it, plain and simple.

"Marv always enlightened us on a lot of things, including the English language and history. Marv was a great orchestrator of men."

Talley also believes that the Bills were also like a family. "A very normal family, one that could get along with each other one moment and maybe fight with each other the next," stated Talley. "We were a tight-knit group of players. And we argued a lot as a group. But that's where Marv came in again. He would let things go just so far, and then he would somehow put a lid on things and calm everybody down."

The Bills of 1990-93, who won four straight American Football Conference titles in a row and went to four straight Super Bowls in a row as well, were a unique team, according to Talley.

"Winning four straight AFC titles and going to four straight Super Bowls is something you may never see again," said Talley. "But I'm not saying it won't happen again. But if another team does it, it will be awfully tough to accomplish. Things have changed in the NFL, especially with free agency. But I think it's the fact of how we won that is so unique during that span of time. I don't think it was a case of being cocky.

"It was the fact that we had a lot of confidence as a team. We would walk out on any football field and know that we could win the game. Even if we were behind, we knew that we could win. We never gave up. I just don't know if teams today could do that or have that much confidence."

One of the most memorable contests Talley played in was the 1991 AFC championship game against the Los Angeles Raiders. The Bills won, 51-3, with Talley recording two interceptions and taking one back for a touchdown. But Talley will be the first to tell anyone that the toughest opponent he ever played against was the Miami Dolphins.

"It was a great rivalry," commented Talley. "I've never seen two teams always play harder against each other than the Bills and Dolphins did when they got together. And for me it became even more intensified because Danny Marino was quarterback. He was one of the toughest quarterbacks to defend against. It was just intense."

Talley has many fond memories of his days in Buffalo.

"Buffalo was like a second home to me," concluded Talley, who was named to the Bills Hall of Fame in 2003. "The fans there are great and love their football team. We had a great run while I played there. And we had a lot of great players come out that team."

"The thing to remember about the Bills of the 1990s was the fact that leadership didn't come from just one player. It came from different guys each week. We always took it game by game as far as leadership went. We weren't always looking for one or two individuals to always make the big plays. It just seemed like somebody new always came up every week to come through for us. I think that's what made us so unique."

While many may agree, Tasker summed it up best for the defense.

"While guys like Bruce Smith and others seemed to come up with the big plays, you could always bet that Darryl was close by or right in the middle of things. He just seemed to be everywhere on defense."

THURMAN THOMAS

WHILE THURMAN THOMAS MAY go down in NFL history as one of the league's top rushers, his performance in an AFC divisional playoff game on January 6, 1990 vs. the Cleveland Browns showed his true versatility as a running back.

Although the Buffalo Bills lost to the Browns, 34-30, and the game went down to the last play, Thomas tied an NFL playoff mark, catching 13 passes. The record had been held by Kellen Winslow of the San Diego Chargers. Thomas totaled 150 yards receiving, including 123 of them on 11 second-half catches.

But it wasn't enough that day as the Bills lost to the Browns in Cleveland. "I'd rather lose a game 34-0, because when you lose like that, you know you never had a chance, but we had a chance," commented Thomas, who

played for the Bills for 12 seasons, 1988-99. "It really hurts to lose a close game like this."

The Bills had opened up an early first-quarter 7-0 lead on a 72-yard pass from quarterback Jim Kelly to wide receiver Andre Reed. Following a first-quarter Matt Bahr field goal for Cleveland, the Browns took the lead, 10-7, in the second quarter when quarterback Bernie Kosar hit Webster Slaughter for a 52-yard TD.

Buffalo came right back five plays later and took a 14-10 lead as Kelly connected with James Lofton for a 33-yard scoring play. The Browns closed out the scoring in the first half when Kosar threw a three-yard scoring pass to Ron Middleton with just six seconds left to give Cleveland the lead, 17-14. When Kosar hit Slaughter on a 44-yard scoring strike, the Browns led, 24-14. Then Thomas

finally got untracked, helping the Bills on their scoring drive. He caught an important 15-yard pass on a third-and-eight situation for the Bills that took the ball to the Browns' four-yard line. Thomas ended up scoring on a six-yard pass play from Kelly to bring the Bills within three, 24-21.

The Bills were still celebrating on the sidelines as the Browns' Eric Metcalf ripped right up the middle to run the kickoff back 90 yards for a TD and give Cleveland a 31-21 third-quarter lead.

Buffalo came right back with a Scott Norwood field goal to open the fourth quarter, which was highlighted by a 27-yard reception by Thomas on a third-and-ten situation. Cleveland came right back and matched field goals with a Bahr 47-yarder to keep the Browns ahead, 34-24.

But the Bills refused to quit. Kelly hit on seven of eight passes on a 77-yard drive that was capped off with a three-yard TD pass to, you guessed it, Thomas. Norwood missed the extra-point kick due to poor field conditions.

The Bills' defense held and got the ball back to their offensive unit on the Buffalo 26 with 2:41 left. Thomas caught two passes in the drive for 20 yards. But it was not enough as Buffalo running back Ronnie Harmon had a pass bounce off his hands in the end zone. On the next play Kelly threw an interception to the Browns' Clay Matthews.

"I thought I was open for a second," said Thomas. "Jim read the coverage before the snap, which a quarterback is supposed to do, and he thought I'd be open. Give Matthews credit, he made a great play."

"That was the thing I always enjoyed about Thurman," said Marv Levy, his former coach with the Bills. "He could do a little bit of everything on offense. He could run with the ball and he could also catch the ball coming out of the backfield. That made him a double threat for us on offense. He could run very well and seemed to evade the defense when needed.

"He had great balance as well. You hit him, and you would just knock him sideways. He could easily regain his balance when he was hit, and find holes to go through or defensive players to go around. He was truly an amazing athlete."

For four straight seasons, 1989-92, Thomas led the NFL in total yards gained from scrimmage. It is considered an unprecedented feat in NFL history. When he combined for 2,038 yards rushing and receiving in 1991 he was named the league's MVP. Thomas passed O. J. Simpson as the team's all-time rushing leader in 1996.

"It's hard to believe what I've accomplished in my career," commented Thomas. "I would have never believed that I would pass somebody like O. J. on the all-time rushing mark."

Thomas had one of his greatest games in the AFC championship game of 1991. It took 24 years to do it, but the Buffalo Bills finally got their shot at going to the Super Bowl. And they did it on January 20, 1991, in one of the most stunning performances in Bills history.

The game turned out to be a rout, as the Bills crushed the Los Angeles Raiders, 51-3, earning a trip to Super Bowl XXV. The game saw several postseason records tied or broken. The Bills tied an AFC/AFL record for most points scored by one team in a championship game (the San Diego Chargers scored 51 in 1963).

The 41 points scored by Buffalo in the first half were a new record, as was Jim Kelly's 73.9 completion percentage and the Bills' 30 first downs. Between the two teams, 18 championship records were broken.

But the game was really secondary to what was happening around the world. The United States had gotten involved in the Persian Gulf War against Iraq. Many football fans came to the game carrying American flags to show their support for the American troops.

The Bills had taken their opening kickoff and went immediately to their no-huddle offense. They drove 75 yards on nine plays, capped off by Kelly's TD pass to wide receiver James Lofton. The Raiders closed the gap to 7-3 on the next series of plays. But the Bills came right back on the next kickoff. Kelly hit Lofton for 41 yards. Two plays later running back Thurman Thomas scored and the rout was on. For the game Thomas rushed the ball for 138 yards, while Kelly passed it for 300 more. Lofton caught five passes for 113 yards.

"I think it was quite an emotional game for everyone concerned," recalled Lofton. "I remember coming out onto the field before the game started and seeing all the American flags. What a sight. As for the game itself, the Bills had everything going for themselves. We could do nothing wrong. Jim [Kelly] was as sharp as I've ever seen him with his passing. And our defense just ran all over the Raiders."

For Bills linebacker Carlton Bailey, the game was very emotional because his father was serving in the Persian Gulf at the time.

"All I remember being told was that the game was going to be televised in Saudi Arabia," said Bailey. "I was just hoping that my dad would be able to see me play. I knew I was going to give it everything; I had to make my dad as proud of me as I was of him."

Following that contest, Thomas led his Bills into Super Bowl XXV. In one of the more memorable Super Bowls, the Bills lost to the New York Giants, 20-19. They had a chance to win the game, but Bills placekicker Scott Norwood's kick in the final seconds of the contest sailed wide right.

Thomas had a memorable game, gaining almost 190 total yards rushing and receiving. The Buffalo passing attack had been shut down. So Thomas took on the Giants single-handedly. Kelly just kept calling his number over and over again in the second half. Unfortunately it wasn't enough for the Bills. He was in line for the game's MVP until Norwood missed his kick.

"Thomas's performance in that game showed how valuable he was to the Bills," commented teammate Steve Tasker. "He could do it all for us. He could carry the Bills if he had to, which he did sometimes. It's just too bad that we fell short as a team with the effort he had in that Super Bowl against the Giants. Thurman was a great athlete. One of the all-time greats in the game. And we were fortunate to have him."

Thomas was recognized for his football accomplishments with his election to the Pro Football Hall of Fame in Canton, Ohio, in 2007.

"It is something you never think about when you are playing," said Thomas, who was also elected to the College Football Hall of Fame in 2008. "It's great to see that so many of us from those Bills teams of the late '80s and early '90s are now being recognized.

"We had some great times. We had some great teams.

"My only regret is that we never won a Super Bowl. But to still get there four straight times, I don't think you will ever see another team do that.

"Despite everything, I'm still proud of the team's accomplishments and being a part of it."

VAN MILLER

ON OCTOBER 14, 2014 Van Miller was added to the Buffalo Bills Wall of Fame. Following the Bills game that day, Miller was escorted to a parking lot where his car was kept.

Several fans approached him, asking Miller for his autograph and posing with him for a photo. Miller signs an autograph, smiles and poses for several photos, talks to the fans and then continues on to a vehicle awaiting to take him to his home.

Miller is truly a legend in Bills football history.

For 37 seasons Miller has been the radio play-by-play announcer for Buffalo's National Football League franchise.

The native of Dunkirk, New York, who is the retired sports director of WIVB-TV in Buffalo, broadcast the Bills first game in 1960. Miller continued calling the Bills' action until 1971. He returned to the broadcast booth in 1979 and has been the "Voice of the Bills" ever since.

Miller will be the first to admit that he has received a few breaks along the way, especially when he initially landed the play-by-play job.

"Dick Gallagher was in my corner," recalled Miller. "WBEN had gone after the games to broadcast them. Gallagher liked me. And you have to remember that I was a young guy at the time and there were some other veteran broadcasters in the area that could have gotten the job.

"In the end the Bills selected me."

Four decades later Miller is still popular with the fans. The veteran radio announcer recalled those early days with the Bills in the American Football League.

"In those first few seasons I did everything alone," remembered Miller. "I did the pre-game, the game and the postgame reports.

"I remember the first time we played the New York Titans in New York's old Polo Grounds. They had to be positioned in the end zone behind the goal posts. Ironically, all the points were scored at the other end of the field.

"We did some other crazy things, too. When we went on our West Coast road swing to play the Denver Broncos, Oakland Raiders and San Diego Chargers, we would be gone from home for better than two weeks. The Bills didn't have the travel budgets that are in place today. So I would have to pack for two weeks and do all my work on the road. It was certainly different than it is today."

Miller, who has broadcast baseball, basketball, soccer and even a soapbox derby or two, admits that football is special.

"Every game is big," stated Miller. "Football is a once-a-week event. Everyone focuses in on the game. And I don't think there is another city in North America that embraces a team the way Buffalo does with the Bills. The impact of this team on the city is mind-boggling."

The broadcast veteran admits while the game may not have changed much, the players have.

"In the early days of the Bills, some of the players would stop over at the house for a beer or something to eat," said Miller. "Others would bring their wives and families over with mine and play cards or just talk. It was much different back in the '60s than today.

"Now the players don't have time for things like that. I give them their space. I'm still close to some of them, but not like with the Bills of the old AFL days."

Miller has certainly seen his share of great Bills moments over 37 seasons. Surprisingly, he was able to select his top five of all time:

1—The Comeback Game (January 3, 1993 at Rich Stadium). "Who could ever forget that game? This was a team down by 32 points in the third quarter and came back to win. Truly one of the greatest moments in the history of pro football."

2—The Bills' first AFL championship game (December 26, 1964). "The Bills won their first AFL championship, defeating the San Diego Chargers, 20-7. The big moment of that game came on the Chargers' second possession when the Bills' Mike Stratton crushed Chargers running back, Keith Lincoln. The hit put Lincoln out of the game and the Bills in control."

3—The first Super Bowl for the Bills (Super Bowl XXV, January 27, 1991). "This is the game that longtime Bills fans had been waiting for. In the end, this is a game that the Bills should have won."

4—The AFC championship game prior to Super Bowl XXV (January 20, 1991). "The Bills crushed the L.A. Raiders, 51-3. It was one of the most perfect contests I've ever seen the Bills play. They could do no wrong on that day."

5—The Bills beat the Jets, 9-6, to clinch the AFC East title (November 20, 1988). "Scott Norwood kicks the winning field goal in OT to win it. The fans came out on the field and tore down one of the goal posts and took one of the uprights up to Ralph Wilson's luxury box."

When it comes to Wilson, Miller has a special place in his heart for the only owner the Bills have ever had.

"Ten years before the Knox Brothers took a chance on an NHL franchise and Paul Snyder did the same with an NBA franchise, an out-of-towner by the name of Ralph Wilson took a chance on Buffalo," commented Miller.

"Ralph Wilson alone made Buffalo a big-league city. He's always reached into his pocket to sign the superstars. I have the deepest admiration for him and the utmost respect."

Miller also has his list of memorable players.

"Cookie Gilchrist was the worst poker player in the history of the NFL," joked Miller. "He would keep going no matter how much he was losing. But Cookie was a sharp guy and player. It would have been great to see him in the same backfield as Thurman Thomas.

"I'll always remember Joe Ferguson as being a total gentleman. And, of course, there is always the late Tom Sestak. Tom was truly a great player and person."

Miller also has his views of broadcasting.

"I've always prided myself on my objectivity," said Miller. "I try to be enthusiastic for both teams. I don't think of myself as a homer. To me, the game is the main object. I've always tried to paint a word picture. I think that's why I've always loved radio. There is room for creativity on radio. I can only watch the ball. That's why I have a guy like Murph [John Murphy] doing color. I think he's the best in the business today. Nobody works harder to prepare for a game than John."

"In 2004 the Pro Football Hall of Fame presented Miller with its Pete Rozelle Radio-Television Award. He was also inducted into the Buffalo Broadcasting Hall of Fame, Greater Buffalo Sports Hall of Fame and the Chautauqua Sports Hall of Fame."

Miller also knows how lucky he is.

"I'm very fortunate to be one of just 32 guys in the U.S. to say that I'm a voice of an NFL team," concluded Miller.

And Buffalo has been very fortunate to have Miller as one of those 32.

ED ABRAMOSKI

"EDDIE ABRAMOSKI WAS PROB- ably the best friend any player who ever played for the Buffalo Bills had. He may have been the trainer, but to the players he was a trusted friend." Those comments made by former Buffalo Bills guard and Hall of Famer Billy Shaw sum up the feelings of any Bills player who played for the team between 1960 and 1995. On Sunday, September 19, 1999, Abramoski was rewarded for his efforts when he was added to the Bills' prestigious Wall of Fame.

For 36 seasons "Abe" served as the team's athletic trainer, joining the team in its initial season in the American Football League in 1960. Abramoski remembers that first year as though it was yesterday.

"It was March of 1960 and Buster Ramsey called me," recalled Abramoski. "Buster had been the Detroit Lions' defensive coordinator when I was there working part-time for the team. He had been hired to coach the Bills that first season. When he asked me if I wanted to come to Buffalo, I didn't have to think twice about it. I thought it would be a great stepping stone for me. I never dreamed that I would be there for as long as I was.

"I was blessed with Mr. [Ralph] Wilson [Bills owner]. I just kept my nose clean and worked hard. And I guess good things would come if I did the things I was supposed to do. And what a great ride it was."

Abramoski talked about the day he was elected to the Bills' Wall of Fame.

"I remember the first day we arrived for our first training camp in East Aurora," said the Erie, Pennsylvania, native. "The football helmets didn't come in until six o'clock the night before we were to begin practice. The equipment man and I stayed up all night putting the facemasks on and getting those helmets ready."

The Bills' former trainer saw it all during the team's first 36 seasons of play. Abramoski was able to narrow down some of his more memorable moments.

"The four Super Bowls in a row that the team went to in the early 1990s is something I don't think any other team will ever be able to repeat," commented Abramoski, who has a bachelor's and master's degree from Purdue University. "And I truly believe that had we beat those New York Giants in that first Super Bowl we went to, I think people would have been talking about a football dynasty like the Pittsburgh Steelers and San Francisco 49ers. I think we were truly a better team than the Giants. But to go to four Super Bowls in a row, I don't think you'll ever see that again."

Abramoski was also quick to point out that he was a part of the two AFL championship Bills teams of 1964 and 1965.

"I was on the committee that is appointed to select that person," said Abramoski, who is also a member of the National Athletic Trainers Hall of Fame and Greater Buffalo Sports Hall of Fame. "They somehow managed to get me out of the room when the vote was taken on who was to go on the Wall this year. When I came back in they said that they had a candidate and it was unanimous. I said that if it was unanimous, who did I vote for? And Mr. Wilson said, you. It brought tears to my eyes. I think there are other guys who are more deserving. All I can say is God bless the committee."

Abramoski recalled some of his early days with the Bills and the AFL.

"Nobody can take that away from us either," added Abramoski. "There were some great guys from that era that played some great football. There were the Strattons, McDoles, Dunaways, Kemps and Sestaks. It was a great era of football."

One player who is very close to Abe's heart from that era is Shaw. The former Bills guard selected Abramoski to present him at his induction ceremonies in Canton, Ohio. It marked the first time an athletic trainer had ever presented a Hall of Fame candidate.

When Abramoski presented Shaw, he spoke of the dedication the Hall of Fame guard had as a player.

"Billy was a trainer's dream," commented Abramoski, who today is retired and resides in Amherst, where he raises racing pigeons. "He lost part of the 1967 season to a severe

"Eddie would **work you hard** when trying to get you back into the lineup. And there was a good chance you might get mad at him. But in the end he was **doing what was best** for you."

—DEFENSIVE END TOM DAY

knee injury. Billy made it back on the field much sooner than our medical staff had anticipated. In those days, following knee surgery, it was a common practice to put a player's knee in a cast for six weeks or so. When we removed Billy's cast, his knee had only 15 degrees of motion. He looked up at the doctor and said, 'How soon can I start working out to build up the muscle around the knee?'

"The doctor told him as soon as he had full motion of his knee back, the exercise program could begin. Billy came back the next day with a good range of motion. He asked me, 'Abe, when do we begin the weights?' Befuddled, I looked at him and said Billy, how did you accomplish this overnight? He told me that he had put his young daughter on his ankle. He lifted her up like a seesaw

until the motion came back. This clearly indicated the drive and dedication that Billy had then and has now."

The late Tom Day, who played defensive end on those same AFL championship Bills teams, summed Abramoski up best.

"Eddie would work you hard when trying to get you back into the lineup," said Day. "And there was a good chance you might get mad at him. But in the end he was doing what was best for you. Abe always looked out for the players. And I think the players always looked up to Eddie to take care of them. He was, and still is, a good friend to all of us."

ERNIE WARLICK

Not a soul in the world was happier than former Buffalo Bills tight end Ernie Warlick when former Baltimore Colts tight end John Mackey was inducted into the Pro Football Hall of Fame.

"Sure, a lot of that had to do with the fact that I was a tight end myself," said Warlick. "But it did my heart good to see any tight end going into the Hall.

"All I could say is that they finally got a tight end into that Hall. And he deserved it.

"John was one of the best."

Warlick's professional football career lasted nine seasons, four with the Bills (1962-65) and five with the Canadian Football League. The Hickory, North Carolina, native made such an impression with the Bills and their fans as a tight end that he was named to the team's 25th Anniversary Club.

"That was really a nice honor," recalled Warlick. "I really enjoyed my few short years that I spent with the Bills.

"They were great, to say the least."

It took quite some time before Warlick arrived on the Western New York scene. Following a four-year stint in the United States Air Force and another five years with the CFL, Warlick joined the Bills in 1962.

"I had never been to Buffalo before," said Warlick. "In fact, I really didn't know too much about the city or the area.

"But I was confident that I would make the team. I was so confident in that belief that I had my family and all our belongings moved to Buffalo before that 1962 season began."

It didn't take long before the Warlick piece of the Bills championship team's puzzle fit into place. The North Carolina Central College graduate recalled the quarterback situation in which the Bills eventually found themselves, with Jack Kemp and Daryle Lamonica.

"There was always a difference between the two," remembered Warlick. "Jack threw a harder ball than Daryle did.

"Jack could really throw that ball. And it was my job to help try and protect the quarterback on passing plays.

"But there would be those particular plays with Jack where somebody would get on him. And then he would turn around and say to me in the huddle, 'Ernie!' And I would say, 'yes Jack, I know. Block.'

"End of conversation."

Warlick went on to compare the two quarterbacks the Bills had during those championship years of 1964-66.

"Daryle would always ask for a commitment from the players in the huddle," said Warlick. "Jack just directed the team with confidence.

"He really didn't have to say anything. That's just the kind of leadership he ran the club with."

AP Photo/Bill Chaplis

Although Warlick never caught that many passes or scored that many touchdowns with the Bills, he still was considered to be an important part of that team. The former tight end recalled the 1965 season, his last in professional football, with fondness.

"That 1965 season was a strange one for me," stated Warlick. "Coach (Lou) Saban had put me on the bench midway through that year.

"I really didn't know why at the time, nor do I really know today. All I know is that I watched a lot of games from the sidelines that year.

"That is, until we got to the championship game against the San Diego Chargers. Just before the start of the game Lou came over to me and told me that I was starting.

"I couldn't believe it. But I went in there and played the game.

"And the thing I remember most about that game is that I scored the first touchdown of the day for the Bills (on a 18-yard pass from Kemp). We went on to win that game and our second straight American Football League Championship."

Following his retirement from pro football, Warlick remained in the Buffalo area, living in Williamsville until his death. The player they called "Hands" died in 2012 at the age of 80.

For years he was a regional sales representative for Chromate Industrial Corporation and travelled throughout Western New York, Pennsylvania and Ohio.

But despite his good fortune in professional football, Warlick still had one regret.

"I went into the 1966 season figuring I would be back with the Bills," recalled Warlick. "Instead, I was cut.

"I had a bad taste in my mouth about that. I could have gone to Miami and played with the Dolphins, who were just an expansion team at the time.

"But I was mad and upset. Unfortunately for me, I was three games short of qualifying for my pension.

"Instead, I went into broadcasting at the time with WGR (now WGRZ), Channel 2. I was there for three years."

But as was Warlick's nature, he could still make something good out of a bad situation.

"I still consider the '64 and '65 championship seasons the most pleasing moments of my professional life," concluded Warlick. "How many people can say that they were part of a championship team?

"And despite the fact that I left football after the 1965 season, I can still say that I left on a winning note.

"After all, how many other people can say they retired from the sport they were playing in on a championship team? I can, and I'm proud of it.

"Maybe I didn't have my pension. But I do have those championships.

"Nobody can take that from me."

And nobody ever did.

TOM DAY

There is a story that the late Tom Day told many times. It seems that Day was having his hair cut one day in the early 1990s at the Metropolitan Barber Shop on Jefferson Avenue in Buffalo.

While Day was sitting in the barber's chair, Bills wide receiver James Lofton (who played for the Bills from 1989-92) entered the shop. Lofton introduced himself to the veteran receiver.

It turned out to be a moment Day wouldn't forget.

"When I told him who I was, Lofton jokingly said, 'Oh, you're one of the old guys,'" recalled Day. "We continued talking until he noticed the championship ring I was wearing.

"He just looked at it and stared. He didn't say a word.

"He just seemed to be in awe of that ring. That's when it occurred to me that that was the one thing he hadn't gotten in his career at that point in time.

"That's why I've always said that you can pay all these players all the money in the world. But it's the ring that does the thing."

Day played nine seasons (1960-68) in the National and American Football Leagues for the Bills, San Diego Chargers and St. Louis Cardinals. Although he was primarily a defensive end, Day did play at offensive guard, as well as defensive and offensive tackle positions during his career.

Following his rookie campaign with the Cardinals in the NFL, Day jumped to the Bills in 1961 and spent seven of his next eight seasons in a Bills uniform.

It was during that period of time that the Bills united the forces of Day, Ron McDole, Tom Sestak and Jim Dunaway to form the front four of the Buffalo defensive unit.

We worked very well together," said Day. "Lou Saban had us believing that the defense would win the games for the team.

"And we believed that. And we worked so well together that we knew each other's moves.

AP Photo/Bill Sikes

"We even had a saying that went, 'Meet you in the backfield.' And we each had our own routes to follow to get to the quarterbacks."

Of course Day was always the first to admit that those routes were not always easy to get through or around.

"The three toughest guys I had to go up against were Ernie Wright of the (San Diego) Chargers, Jim Tyler of the (Kansas City) Chiefs and Winston Hill of the (New York) Jets," stated Day.

"Wright was the toughest of the three. You had to use physical force to get around him. Hill would do anything to stop me.

Anything. And Tyler, well, I would talk him to death. I just talked to him all the time.

"He called me a chatter box. I would talk to him all the time just to distract him so I could get to Len Dawson easier.

"And he couldn't stop me from talking."

Despite the two championship teams Day played on for the Bills, the former defensive end's most memorable day as a player came as a member of the Chargers in 1967. It happened just prior to the start of the game against the Bills on Day's first return visit to War Memorial Stadium.

"When I was first introduced that day, the Bills fans gave me a five-minute standing ovation," stated Day. "There were over 42,000 fans there that day.

"Now I had won honors in high school, was an All-American in college and had even been an All-Pro as a professional.

"But nothing ever topped that standing ovation I got from the Bills fans. And even though I was wearing a Chargers uniform I still considered myself a Bill."

Once retired from football, Day still was involved with the game. He worked with retired and active players from the NFL Players Association as a counselor.

To the day he died, Day always had the same philosophy about pro football in Buffalo.

"Once a Bill, always a Bill," said Day, who passed away in August of 2000. "It doesn't matter if you're a hundred years old.

"Once people find out that you played for the Bills, they don't forget."

TERRY PEGULA

"My name is Terry Pegula and the Pegulas just bought a football team. We all just bought a team, our team, the Buffalo Bills.

"And the name of our team will not change, it will stay the Buffalo Bills."

That is how Terrence M. "Terry" Pegula opened his mid-October 2014 press conference inside the Bills practice facility. Just a month earlier the National Football League announced that Pegula had the winning bid to purchase the NFL's Buffalo franchise.

The team had been placed up for sale following the March 25, 2014 death of Ralph Wilson, the only owner the Bills had ever known. In the months that followed Wilson's passing, Bills fans were kept on pins and needles, not knowing whom the new team owner would be.

Real estate mogul Donald Trump, as well as a group from Toronto headed by musician Jon Bon Jovi, had also submitted bids. Western New Yorkers were so upset with Bon Jovi that some radio stations would not play his music on the air.

Pegula actually found out just what the Bills mean to the Western New York area on a trip back from Michigan in mid-September. While the NFL had already chosen his bid to purchase the Bills, Pegula discovered what a valuable asset the Bills are to Buffalo.

"Coming back from Traverse City (Michigan) and listening to the radio, listening to fans, I don't think any of us realized the fear that they had in their hearts that they were going to lose their Bills," said Pegula.

The new Bills owner continued at his press conference, "I was humbled by you, the fans, with the outpouring of emotion that I saw when our name was announced as the winner of the bid. I know there's been comments about how much I paid for the team ($1.4 billion).

"I want to ask our fans if I overpaid, because I know what they're going to tell you."

The Bills are not the first pro sports team in which Pegula has invested. In February of 2011 Pegula purchased the Buffalo Sabres of the National Hockey League and the Buffalo Bandits of the National Lacrosse League for $189 million.

Three months later he purchased the Rochester Americans of the American Hockey League and today serves as the minor league affiliate of the Sabres.

In addition, Pegula won the development rights to the Webster Block located on the Buffalo waterfront. In November 2014 HarborCenter opened, which features two hockey rinks, a parking garage, restaurants and a hotel to open in 2015. It is located right across the street from the First Niagara Center, home of the Sabres.

To say that Pegula has pumped energy into the city of Buffalo is an understatement. People are jumping on the bandwagon for the revitalization of Buffalo.

Many are now calling that area of Buffalo, "Pegulaville."

Born in Carbondale, Pennsylvania, Pegula's story is one that reflects the true American Dream. After borrowing $7500 from family

Janet Schultz Photography

and friends, Pegula founded East Resources, a natural gas drilling company, in 1983.

The company became very successful, and consequently Pegula became a multi-billionaire. As of September 2014 his net worth was estimated at $4.6 billion.

Pegula's purchase of the Bills is probably one of the biggest stories in the history of Buffalo. The day the press conference was held, it was broadcast live on local television and radio stations and was attended by not only local and national media but also local politicians, businessmen and players, past and present, of the Bills.

Interestingly, Pegula's wife, Kim, did not join her husband on the stage set up for the press conference. Instead, she sat in the front row with the Pegula children.

Pegula addressed the issue of Kim's role with the Bills.

"We're both owners," he said. "She will put her touch on the organization in her own way and that will be a nice thing, and she has a good business mind, too.

"She will be involved, she's part owner."

Bills president, Russ Brandon, summed up the news of the new ownership.

"It is certainly a great time to be a Buffalonian," remarked Brandon.

But perhaps Pegula summed it up even better.

"Owning any professional team is about winning, and the primary goal of our ownership will be to win the Super Bowl and bring championships to the city of Buffalo.

"We want to bring a Super Bowl to the Niagara region, courtesy of your, our, my, Buffalo Bills."